MAGIC GARDENS

MAGIC GARDENS
(or the starry-eyed saviours of the western night)

by Viva Las Vegas

FACTORY GIRL PRESS

to every naked girl, ever

Introduction: On Salvation

My decision to move to Portland was like a game of pin the tail on the donkey. I blindfolded myself, ran at the wall, and shoved a pushpin in the ass of America.

Less than two months before, I'd been in New England, sweating under a polyester graduation gown while George Bush the First admonished the members of my class to pursue their dreams. For most of my peers that meant donning suits and ties and commuting to sterile offices in order to keep the status quo chugging along. But for me it meant something else; for me it meant anything else.

Up on the dais to collect my diploma, I looked George square in the eye as I shook his hand and thanked him for his address. I wanted him to know that I'd heard him loud and clear. From that day forward I was done with the gifted and talented program and was going to do whatever the fuck I wanted.

My poor parents beamed unsuspectingly from the audience. The eldest of their four children, I was anything but easy. Still I'd managed to become valedictorian of my high school class and, now, a graduate of Williams College. I was a health nut and even made it to church half a dozen times a year. For all my agonizing growing pains, I appeared to be turning out quite nicely. Mom and Dad probably thought I was going to get a nice job, meet a nice man, and have a nice life. They should have known better.

My dad is a preacher. My mom is a teacher. They gave me heaven and earth. By the time I was out of their house I'd lived on four continents, spoke five languages, and had learned to look for beauty, truth, and salvation in all things. I knew that my sole responsibility on this earth was to let my little light shine. It seemed a no-brainer to me that my little light would shine brightest, was most needed, in the darker corners of life. I don't think it's surprising at all that I ended up naked, glowing, incandescent in one of the darkest corners imaginable.

* * *

So many colors make up the everyday wash of appointments and moorings. During the day, the huge white light from the sky dilutes them all. The green palm trees, pink pigs, and purple elephants look sickly in the sun with their faded paint and broken bulbs. But at night they're tarted up like the perfect whore. At night the giant neon signs on North Interstate promise a life that throbs and crackles and doesn't disappoint. At night the electric lights fire up and taunt God with an energy and perfection born of our gluttony, our devotion to extravagance, our fear of nothingness.

The West was founded on the promise of easy money, and its most successful citizens are still its outlaws, shysters, and thieves. Pornographers find especially fertile ground here, and so do titty bars. Portland, with its endlessly gray, wet neon night, has held the title of "most strip clubs per capita" for well over two decades. Most of the bars are housed in grungy clapboard or cement hovels on the outskirts of town. They are warm, welcoming places in the midst of a depressed and lonely collective consciousness. With names like Beavers, Jiggles, Roosters, and Bottoms Up, they don't promise much. But in this industry, you don't need to. Sex sells. Add beer and you sell more.

Everything looks pretty surreal when there's a real live naked woman onstage. Suddenly you've transcended polite society; protocol is refreshingly warped. It's exciting, possibly dangerous. Everywhere there are mirrors, reflections of you, of her. Plumes of cigarette smoke give shape to breath, to words. The nicotine haze adds to the subterranean surrealism. Everyone is alone—pondering the dancer or his drink. Life's traumas and dramas ebb and flow in consciousness as dancers come and go. Some mesmerize completely, and everything else falls away.

Get a whiskey with a beer back. Light up a smoke. Sit at the rack...

So many girls pass through this crucible. They are perfectly ripe, teetering on the brink of hard-won maturity but not yet sullied by that certain cynicism that rains from heaven when you are precisely twenty-three and three-quarters. So many girls enter this industry pretty and hopeful beyond belief. Freshly weaned from troubled adolescences, they giggle and smile and wiggle out of their panties, and overnight realize they have the world by the balls. The tricky thing is knowing what to do with it.

There was this curve of a back in a deadbeat Western town
on a wet night in a smoke-choked Chinatown
There was this curve of a back reflected in the glass
reflected in the glass reflected in the glass
This curve of a back slowly snaked down to the ground and hid
under a smooth creamy belly and an arabesque of a throat
This curve of a back arched on the floor, lips spread in pleasure
body twisting slowly...
So beautiful in the light I thought my heart would break
and the world would be saved entire.

Welcome to Pornland

I lit a cigarette and eyed the junky, mustard-yellow Victorian boarding house from across the street. I'd been pounding the pavement all day in the searing August heat, meeting building managers and touring nice normal studios for rent. But I kept coming back to the Lawn Apartments.

"This place is totally beat," I said, just to hear myself talk.

The sky clouded over suddenly and an angry little thunderstorm broke. A woman in a short white skirt, nylons, dirty white heels, and a faux fur coat raced by. She wore ribbons wrapped around her pigtails like a Valley Girl, but her grisly expression shot the whole look to pieces. A little ways behind her followed a younger black man in a Chicago Cubs nylon jacket, visibly seething. This neighborhood—once pretty tony, judging by the dilapidated Victorians and gothic mansions—was now the provenance of pros, pimps, and pushers. Bums slept out the midday shower on the steps of the old cathedral.

I sucked down the last of my cigarette and turned my attention back to the house. It was enormous and awkward looking, three stories high with gables poking out in every direction. Some of the windows were broken and sections of the moss-covered roof looked ready to fall into the street. Hippie doodads peeked out of garrets. A row of chairs and a beat-up old guitar hung out uneasily on the second balcony. The place appeared, frankly, uninhabitable. The only thing that looked stable at all was the orange and black FOR RENT sign in the window.

I crossed 18th Avenue and climbed up the heavily warped and broken steps to the rickety, sloping porch, the hundred-year-old wood rotted by so much rain. A cat piss-mildew perfume accosted me in the doorway.

The lobby's carpet was threadbare and stained. Bits of crumbling plaster showed through where years of paint and ancient flowery wallpaper had fallen away. Along the back wall was a tall row of metal mailboxes, festooned with punk rock stickers. Paintings and anarchist treatises covered the remaining wallspace, and a long string of multicolored origami birds fell three full stories from the top of the stairwell.

In spite of its tiny studios with filthy shared bathrooms and the fact that it looked like it should be condemned, the Lawn was tempting. The front door was always open, so I could waltz right in and explore on my own, undisturbed. After several visits, my nose had become more accustomed to the overwhelming stench that greeted me in the lobby, and tiny little Apartment #2, tucked under the enormous *Gone with the Wind* staircase and vacant except for a sleeping bag in the loft, was really starting to grow on me. In fact, more and more I had my heart set on it, with its fifteen-foot ceilings, bay window converted into a kitchenette, and single bare bulb.

I stood some forty feet under an open skylight and felt the rain on my face. My heart whirred like I was in a sacred place. I knew I was home. I hadn't been home in five years.

The next day I charged an eight-hundred-dollar money order for rent and deposit. Being a college brat had paid off in the end. "This credit card is the only thing separating me from the streets," I mused, laughing off the dread that accompanied signing the receipts. I wouldn't be able to coast on my credit much longer. Then I'd starve, which would be romantic and possibly fruitful in a Henry Miller sort of way.

I headed back to the Lawn, money order and application in hand. Twilight crept across the western hills, turning the magnificent evergreens gray and smoky black, and cloaking the bleak street in gorgeous pinks and yellows. The lovely wash of color made the needle-strewn sidewalks and sad, lonely faces look even more poignant, like hopeless inhabitants on the frontiers of purgatory, heaven so visible, so gorgeous, so pink and yellow and deepening cobalt blue, but just beyond reach and getting further away with every breath.

I walked down to Union Station where I'd stowed my guitar and my bag. Then, with my few possessions and a six-pack of cold beer, I officially moved in.

I played guitar for a while, sitting on the dirty black painted-wood floor, a new pioneer in the age-old idea of the West. Funny I didn't find it hackneyed in the least. I was young and invincible. Anything could happen here. It was the end of the earth, and it was dead beat. The stories I'd seen already in these people's sad faces! There was gold in those hills, I knew it.

Superhero

It wasn't exactly my goal in life to become a stripper, although I had considered it. My goal was to be a musician, maybe the next Bob Dylan or Chrissie Hynde. But destiny intervened and I moved in next door to Portland's most notorious naked chick.

She went by the unlikely name Miss Mona Superhero. More unlikely still, she embodied it. She was tall and proud, full-breasted, long-legged, and bald.

I met her on the front porch of the Lawn. She was wearing mechanic's overalls with a patch over her heart that read "Elvis." The patch should have read "Nastasya Filippovna."

"Who are you?" she sniffed haughtily.

Before I had a chance to answer, a twenty-something skateboarder

COME SEE
Miss Mona's
LADIES OF
LEISURE
CABARET

FEATURING

MISS
MONA
SUPERHERO

JUNE
29TH

joined us on the porch. She struck a flirtatious tone. "Chris, darling! Give me a cigarette?"

"Sorry, Mona. It's my last one."

"Oh no! I really really need a cigarette," she whimpered. "Maybe you could buy us a pack at Elias's?"

"God, Mona. I don't know why I do this shit for you. Anything else?"

"Supersize Big Mac and a strawberry shake."

The boy headed to the corner store and returned soon after with two packs of smokes and a bag from McDonald's. I was embarrassed for him. Little did I know Mona could make puppies of anyone, everyone.

Several days later she knocked on my door. Freshly graduated from a little Ivy that frowned upon any sort of provocative individuality, I was still wearing lots of Patagonia and no mascara. Mona, however, stood at my door regally attired in a floor-length ball gown of peacock-green brocade. Somehow she'd stolen it earlier in the day out of my new-to-me chest of drawers. The dress had come with the drawers, and I'd thought it would make a pair of hideous curtains at best, until I saw her tits bursting out of it.

"Change your clothes," she ordered. "We're going out. You have five minutes."

I stuttered a half-formed excuse to her already-turned back, but the enormous Chinese dragon tattoo that snaked across it only mocked me. Suddenly I was breaking the crust off foundations, eye shadows, and lipsticks I'd had since seventh grade. I couldn't believe Mona's shtick was working on me. Thank God I'd bought a black catsuit earlier that day off the clearance rack at Urban Outfitters. Thank God I owned exactly one pair of black heels.

I followed her breathlessly as we galloped around twilight Portland, shooting pool, stealing drinks, and amassing admirers. Dressed up and messed up, Mona was luminous. She shone brighter than any nightlight in town, and the moths swarmed around obligingly. College jocks toasted us with rounds of Jägermeister and forked over dollars for the jukebox at the Commodore. Drag queens out for a stroll with their beefcake boyfriends catcalled as we sauntered down Stark Street. Greek bar-owners in Old Town plied us with shots of ouzo. All the while the ubiquitous, fat, tattooed Bettie Page look-alikes eyed us warily over the rims of their vintage cat eye glasses, drowning in pints of PBR they'd actually paid for. Eventually we ended up at Magic Gardens.

Mona worked at the Magic—a dive bar in the center of a deserted and dangerous Chinatown. She waltzed through the door as if she were Mozart's Queen of the Night, shoulders back, her voluminous dress frothing about her. I tried my best to ape her bravura. Soon we were sipping strong Jack and Cokes in front of a rapt audience, which Mona regaled with tales of debauchery. Even the stripper stopped stripping in order to fawn over Mona. I sat in stunned silence by her side and hungrily took in my environs.

It appeared that the Magic was only incidentally a strip club. Most of the guys preferred to converse with the barmaid or stare into their beers, occasionally sneaking a glance at the mirrors that reflected the all-nude-girl on the tiny wooden stage. There was threadbare carpet throughout, but it was dark enough that you didn't really notice the patches of wear. The red lights and abundance of reflective surfaces made the whole joint glitter and twinkle like some hallucinated Christmas. A giant neon Viking woman lorded over an indifferent corner right next to the dressing room, literally a hole in the wall screened by a smoke-stained plastic curtain.

Mona got celebrity treatment at the Magic. At least four big guys hovered around, eager to hold back her nonexistent hair as she barfed into the trashcan at the waitress station, looking every bit a vision in that stunning peacock-green brocade ball gown. Eventually one of them carried her to his cab and gave us a free ride home. I was star-struck.

Inexplicably, this prima donna took a liking to me—a scrappy little bird fresh out of rich-kid college—and tucked me under her wing. Again, probably anyone would have done. She needed an audience at all times, and it didn't much matter if it was me or the guy from Apartment #9 newly released from the Tucson mental hospital who accompanied her on her mad, drunken rambles. That I was especially proud to be this audience probably endeared me to her more, and she took me on as a sister.

And so I became Miss Mona's puppy, delightedly trotting after her from bar to bar to trashcan. This lasted for six months, until we were both dead broke and had to get boyfriends. Those were without a doubt the best six months of my life.

Calling All Angels

My credit card was two coffees away from being maxed, so I'd spent a constructive morning distributing resumés downtown. I'd been in Portland almost three weeks, and it was time to bite the bullet and get a job. It was mid-August and oppressively hot. I dressed carefully in my best skateboarder duds: brown Ultrasuede surfer shorts, matching striped bra top and ratty old Vans sneakers. Not exactly an outfit to wear job-hunting, but I didn't exactly want a job.

I was a liberal arts graduate with a degree in anthropology, and was fluent in German and adept at French, Indonesian, and Swahili after two years of study abroad. That meant I was qualified to work at Starbucks and not much else. The fact that I'd graduated from a hotshot East Coast college meant little to nothing on the West Coast. Still I'd somehow managed to track down a few job leads while hanging around pubs and coffee shops—a sales position at a kids' computer company, a design firm that employed an actual anthropologist to predict what people would buy, a couple of temp firms—but I wasn't serious about any of them. The idea of working in an office chilled me to the bone. I honestly felt I'd rather be embalmed.

I returned to the Lawn sweaty and exhausted, planning the afternoon's coffee shop screed on anthropologists who sell their souls to capitalism. I was greeted in the lobby by what looked like a Tupperware party. A dozen people, most of them mostly women, sat chatting around piles of pastel paper. There were two half-eaten pizzas on the stairs, and pot smoke hung thick in the doorway. Mona emerged from her room with her cigarettes.

"Hey, Mo," I said, heading over to the mailboxes. Mine sported a shiny new Melvins sticker.

"Hey. Come join the party. Teresa, give this kid a stapler."

A gorgeous woman bounded over to me, an olive-skinned brunette with huge brown eyes and an even huger smile.

"Hey, Dude! What's up? Wanna join our fold-and-staple party?"

"Uhh—" I was disconcerted by her outsized gestures. Had I been deaf her words would've still been crystal-clear.

COME SEE
Miss Mona's
LADIES OF
LEISURE
CABARET
FEATURING
TERESA
DULCE

JUNE
29TH

BERBATI'S PAN • 231 SW ANKENY

"Here! Grab some pizza and sit down."

She made a place for me in the circle between one of several bull dykes—dressed like a Hasidic Jew—and a lovely blonde woman wearing pink sunglasses. A large pile of orange paper was plunked down in front of me. Before I knew what was going on, the Hasidic dyke handed me a rainbow.

"Put the orange one on top of the pink one," s/he said.

Okay. Done. I passed the stack to the blonde, who put a yellow sheet on top, handed it to a buff Mexican gal who folded the stack and passed it on to Teresa. Teresa stapled the six sheets once in the middle.

Teresa had been printing her stripper zine, *Danzine,* for a little over a year. She solicited articles from strippers, phone sex operators, and peep show performers as well as lawyers, accountants, and public health officials. *Danzine* came out every two or three months and was the nucleus of the growing Portland sex worker political movement.

When we finished folding and stapling the lot, I shyly asked Teresa for a copy of my own. I took it up to my loft, read it cover to cover, then ransacked Mona's apartment for back issues.

The articles ran the gamut from informative harm reduction stuff to sexy fiction. Brandi wrote about working the jackshacks in a hilarious column called "Confessions of a Fantasy Booth Girl." Elinor drew off-color comics of the real world of strippers—a dancing girl imagining a grocery list while the customer imagined she really really liked him. Kennedy wrote a hot bisexual stoner snowboarder fiction serial. Gals contributed travelogues of places they'd stripped, from Aberdeen, Scotland, to Tucson, Arizona. Every issue featured a list of important numbers: abuse, suicide, and AIDS hotlines; doctors; legal assistance; rehab, etc. Women wrote about partner abuse. Teresa wanted to make damn sure her sisters weren't hurt. A Bad Date List was compiled and distributed to all the clubs, warning sex workers of men, cars, and corners to avoid. Eventually this spawned a 24-hour Bad Date Hotline, sponsored by the more legitimate powers that be in a strange marriage of sex workers and the anti-sex-work establishment. Teresa excelled at getting these unnatural partners into bed together.

The idea of a proactive sex worker movement was new to me and totally irresistible. My training in anthropology and sociology had convinced me that what humans wanted and needed more than any-thing was community, and here, in the lobby of my own apartment building, was a blossoming community of brilliant, sexy artists and their support staff. I knew I wanted to join the ranks, whether it was folding and stapling, putting pen to paper, or—maybe someday—doffing my drawers for the cause.

What's in a Name, Part One

Everyone should have a stripper name. It's a touchstone to a new you: a lovely, naughty little mask that you design for youself, an alter ego you can turn on at will, like Clark Kent stepping into a phone booth and emerging as Superman. With a stripper name you can totally reinvent yourself, casting off the various humiliations of your first seventeen to seventy years. It's an escape portal from real life into another more glamorous more vivacious more FREE dimension.

Some say that the false names belie a deeper falseness in the sex industry, and that if you call yourself Lexus or Mercedes you're probably a Honda or Toyota underneath. But the stripper name is really much simpler. It's fun, like putting on makeup. It's also a safety precaution. Some girls intend to run for city council someday, while some are running from the law. Some girls have family in town who might recognize sister Amethyst's name in the industry mags. So Amethyst, a beautiful black economics major matriculated from an Ivy League school, called herself Venus.

Girls who danced by their real names were common enough. Perhaps a quarter of them did away with *noms de guerre*. Maybe they were more self-actualized. Maybe their families lived in faraway burgs. Or maybe they were insipid, uncreative totally nudes. I instantly loved the ruse of the fake name and its chameleonic effect on identity. Still, one ought to choose a stripper name with care, as over time the new persona will morph to suit the name: by the time I met Sugar, twenty years into her career, her hair was still in pigtails and she wore nothing but white.

So, say you grew up in the Bay Area and are of Mexican descent. You went to a top university and are committed to public service and are a selfless superhuman. You've got a smile that could save the world and a big strawberry birthmark on your ass where the angels kissed you. What do you call yourself, Mother Teresa?

Teresa.

Teresa was quite simply a saint. *Danzine* was just the tip of the iceberg; in addition she did HIV outreach, ran needle exchange sites, appeared at public health symposiums, and coordinated art shows to fête her cause: sex work was *work,* and its workers deserved the same respect and rights afforded to other workers. She was single-minded in her sex worker activism and would do whatever it took to get the word out. To that effect she demanded huge favors from everyone, but we were happy to oblige. People like to feel united, working for a common cause. Certain folks would donate pot, others clothes, some rides, some rent. Teresa stripped occasionally, but mostly she lived off the goodwill of others.

Teresa had real bad hooker fashion: too-short, too-tight, high-waisted skirts paired with, say, a rhinestone halter-top. Or her butch look: jeans, t-shirt, no bra, borrowed truck, picking up art, condoms, needles… But once you started talking to her, whether you were the mayor, a mom, or a bum, you caught the fever. She was justice and righteousness wrapped in drop-dead beauty, like an allegorical Renaissance statue come to life, but with a cackle as loud as a military jet. She talked like a sideshow barker, her words peppered with excited "dudes!" and dressed up with wild gestures. She was always laughing, always smiling. It was her way of encouraging people to be optimistic, fabulous, alive. She was infectious. And she could dance like a motherfucker.

Legend had it that Mona and Teresa met at the Yellow Rose, a strip club outside of Austin. Teresa, fresh from the University of California at Berkeley, was a dyed-in-the-wool social activist who knew implicitly that trading sex for money was political. Mona was biding her time, stripping and slamming Bushmills while waiting for the twist of fate that would spring her from Texas for good. Kindred cuckoo geniuses with enormous appetites for pot, the two of them hit it off immediately.

Eventually they left Austin in Teresa's crappy car to see as much of the strip club nation as they could. The car finally ate it in Portland. God breaks down lots of cars in Portland. They'd maxed Teresa's credit cards and couldn't get it fixed, so they stayed. Three years later, when I met them, Teresa was folding and stapling her one-year anniversary issue of *Danzine,* and Mona was staging the first of her soon-to-be-famous cabarets.

Life Oughtta Be a Cabaret

There's so much going on at any given moment that we stubbornly ignore. You have to in order to keep up with the monotonous rituals of civilized life. But sometimes your eyes are forced open, like it or not. Maybe by a car accident, maybe cancer, maybe Mona…

Mona was really peaking when I met her. She was as dysfunctional as they come but had assembled such an array of rent payers, hamburger getters, cigarette lighters, and other lackeys that she was able to create for a short while. What came out of her crazy head played like fully formed David Lynch films—sexy, macabre, and gorgeous. She called them cabarets.

That hot August, Mona was preparing her first cabaret, to be held at the super swank strip bar Club 505 on her twenty-sixth birthday. She'd recruited an army of freaks and losers to hammer nails, spray-paint stuff, and massage her ego. Strange men came by the Lawn with wood and built sets and props. One of her stalkers wired a little robot mask for her. Occasionally you'd hear her scream for more silver spray paint, burst into tears, or ferociously fire a slave or two. The apartments at the Lawn were very small, so this huge construction project took place in the lobby and on the front porch, through which we all had to tiptoe to get to our rooms.

Mona's primary rent guy owned a porn store specializing in Japanese bondage films, vomit and shit fetishes, and animal action. He was a creepy nerd who sported a dark-brown Dutch boy bob and thick Buddy Holly glasses. Occasionally Mo referred to him as her boyfriend. He paid for everything. Took her shopping, bought her fancy shoes, got her laundry done, brought her groceries. Mona simply could not manage these things on her own. Of course she despised the creature and treated him like shit—which he seemed to love—but he was integral in getting Mo out of bed, off the ground, and launched into outer space.

Mo's first cabaret turned my wilted heart into bread dough, kneaded it some, and then let it rise. I'd never seen anything in all my travels that rivaled the dozen naked chicks writhing under Miss Mona's command. Though I all but worshipped Mona for her talent and bravado, I could find her Royal Highness bullshit a bit nauseating. But watching her in action the night of her cabaret, I decided that she deserved the royal treatment. What poise, what tits! And what heart— a little engine that could. Goddamn girl deserved the entire world on a platter. Then she'd hawk loogies at it and laugh laugh laugh.

Club 505 was on the outskirts of town, so I hitched a ride in Tucker's old brown limo along with a bunch of Lawn weirdos. Tucker managed the Lawn. That meant he got to live in his shitty studio for free if he kept at least one of the three communal toilets unplugged. He was a handsome Southern gentleman who wore his long dark brown hair in a ponytail and kept a bucket of freshly roasted peanuts outside his door for us. He was also a heroin addict and had plenty of access to pot. We'd all gotten stoned in the back of the limo—five dudes between thirty-five and sixty and me—so I was really tripping on the glamour of the club when we arrived. It was grand and theatrical, with hundreds and hundreds of lights and a booming sound system and gorgeous women everywhere. It was definitely nothing like the Magic Gardens.

Mona greeted us warmly at the door in a tight red *cheongsam* and sky-high black platform heels. To her left was the dressing room. A phalanx of girls paraded in and out of it, allowing us to glimpse a cacophony of feathers, sequins, and skin as Mona adeptly steered us toward the bar.

The club was huge. In the center was a large hexagonal stage ringed with seats. Tiers of red-covered couches interspersed with little tables rose up on all sides of the room like a fancy Roman coliseum. To the side of the stage was a long bar, on top of which lounged a lithe short-haired blonde wearing a turquoise string bikini.

We staked out a group of empty seats and watched in stoned silence as the club rapidly filled with tattooed rockers and sophisticated downtown types, whose numbers soon overwhelmed the solitary fat guys and little cliques of men in suits—types I figured to be the usual suburban strip club wallpaper. Most of the suits left. Most of the fat guys stayed. Finally the lights grew dim and two dashing emcees in tuxedoes loped onstage. Vinny Cleanhands and Thomas Pancake (where *did* Mona find these people?) performed a masterful Lenny Bruce-style stand-up routine before welcoming us all to Miss Mona's Sex Kitten Cabaret.

Soon all manner of flesh was flashing from the stage: old, young, large, small, boy, girl, black, white, each more fabulous than the last. I caught my first glimpse of Morgan Le Fay with her strong athlete's body, porcelain skin, and Shirley Temple head of black ringlets; six-footer June, who moved her long languid limbs with impossible, mesmerizing grace; and Rain Stormm, a vaguely Cherokee-looking beauty filled with old-fashioned coy and charisma. I moved to the edge of my seat when the emcee announced Teresa. I had only seen her in activist mode, mounting art shows and doing *Danzine*. I couldn't wait to see her dance.

The stage was set as a boudoir for Teresa—draped in sheer curtains and set with a vanity and stool. She glided on in a diaphanous robe with fluffy slippers, accompanied by two big burly men in tuxedoes and Mexican wrestling masks. Lounging happily while an Edith Piaf song played, Teresa slipped out of her robe and did a reverse striptease, assisted by the studs. They slowly rolled her silk stockings up her legs and helped her into a classic hooker outfit—garter belt, skintight miniskirt, and flashy brassiere. She fluffed her hair, powdered her privates, perfumed her pits, and applied bloodred lipstick. The bucks helped her into a little fur and a large feather boa. With a kick of her hips and a knowing glance, she was out the door.

A gal named Lara Lee performed a traditional shove-your-tits-in-my-face bit, but with such wit that it reinvented the genre. Lara had enormous fake breasts and a body that made them look almost natural. She was a big curvy girl with long red hair, tousled and teased à la Barbarella, a playful smirk of a smile, and an infectious stage presence. According to Mona, Lara'd run away from home at age fourteen and had supported herself ever since. Now she was twenty-two, owned her own house, and drove a brand new pickup.

Midway through the show, for half-time entertainment, Lara Lee, Teresa, and several others made titty prints and auctioned them off to high bidders—a fundraiser for *Danzine*. Boobies were lovingly painted blue and then smooshed onto a new Hanes white t-shirt. Voila! The little sex worker zine made dollars aplenty to cover their Kinko's costs and a bag or two of pot.

By now I was suffering from booze/pot-induced vertigo. Instead of watching the performers, I stared hard into the back of Mr. Pink's head, trying to overcome the dizziness that threatened to hurl either me or my guts onto the next tier of seats. Mr. Pink was a misanthropic art punk from Austin and my neighbor at the Lawn. He and Mona and I had hung out a few times together and I had a bit of a crush on him. He had the word "scabby" tattooed on the back of his neck in Old English letters, and I trained my woozy gaze on it until he turned around.

"Hey neighbor. Liking the show so far?"

"It's amazing. I can't believe it," I slurred, desperately racking my brain for something to offer in the way of conversation other than platitudes. Luckily I was saved by a loud hiss from a fog machine. The lights went down and the opening notes of Thomas Dolby's "She Blinded Me with Science" rang through the cavernous space. This had to be Mona. No one else would play such a retarded song.

Suddenly she appeared onstage. Not walked onstage, not crawled, just *appeared*. The haze in my brain cleared in a second. I was transfixed. I couldn't look away.

Her entire body from her stiletto thigh-high boots to her plastic bob wig was painted silver. She stood perfectly still for a full twenty seconds, regal, commanding attention. Soon I would recognize this as her signature move: forcing her victims to look at her before she did them in with some hypnotic Medusa eye contact. This time, however, her eyes were covered by a little blinking LED mask.

Whatever role she had to embody, Mona always morphed completely into character. Tonight she was a super-sexualized Japanese she-bot. I'd noticed several expensive fetish comic books on she-bots lying on her apartment floor, but I hadn't put two and two together until now. She slinked around for a while, emotionless but eerily commanding, and then slowly undid her metal breastplate. Her awesome tits were painted silver, too, and a little control panel blinked red above her heart.

My mouth was completely dry. I sucked the last of the melted ice from my empty Jack-and-Coke. She was the most captivating stage creature I'd ever witnessed, a Sarah Bernhardt for the twentieth century.

She posed and preened, seductively moving through angular robot positions. Finally she undid her utility belt and slowly slid out of her silver hot pants, proudly revealing the biggest thickest forest of silver pubic hair anyone had ever witnessed. The Superhero.

That was it. I was sold. I would be a stripper, too. When later we all piled into the old brown limo for the long ride home, I felt like I was on fire, the brightest star burning like hell in the heavens. My destiny was clear. At least, the next four-or-so years of it was. At least, it was until the next morning, when I soberly decided that I shouldn't give up on a real job just yet.

* * *

I awoke the next day with a start, as some heavy object crashed against the wall that separated Mona's apartment from mine. I threw on a robe and went over to Mona's but was greeted by a locked door, behind which she was howling in existential agony. I whispered through the keyhole, trying to calm her.

"Mona... Mona... Open up. I love you."

I went to Pink's apartment and told him of the crisis we had on our hands. This was not her usual hangover, which could generally be ameliorated with a Happy Meal and a Bloody Mary.

Pink coaxed his way into her room and I followed. She was wrapped in a kimono and lying on the floor, the previous night's eye makeup covering her entire face and neck.

"I WANT TO DIE! I WANT TO DIE!"

There were knives out. Pink calmly gathered them and brought them to his apartment. I found the pot and loaded a bowl.

"Mona, drink this." I held the pipe to her mouth. She hit my hand away.

"I QUIT! I FUCKING QUIT! I want to DIE!"

"Mona! Stop it! You're a fabulously brilliant creature and everyone loves you!"

She collapsed on the floor again, screaming and wailing. I grabbed her address book and made my way through the list of weirdos. I called Mark, the normal graphic designer guy. He came over pronto with comics.

An hour later I peeked in on her. She was curled up in her chair in a fetal position. All the lights were out and a thin bit of August sun made its way through the quilt hung over the bay window. The room was thick with pot smoke. Mark loved Mona. He did all her posters and flyers in the wee wee hours at his office. His designs were awesome—retro and sexy and super-stylish. Mo—who couldn't operate a mouse—claimed she did them all herself.

Mark got Mona down for a nap. We tiptoed around and wrung our hands and spoke in hushed voices until, a couple hours later, a low moan emanated through the wall separating her loft from mine, followed by a heart-stopping scream. Oh, God. Here we go again.

She screamed and sobbed for two days with the door locked. Finally, on the third day, the door to her room was open a crack, the blankets over the window thrown aside, and she was quiet.

I crept in, careful not to upset the calm. I sat on the floor next to her and put my hand on her back, lit her a cigarette, and looked around the room. She had completely destroyed it. Ripped clothes, broken TV, broken dishes, and scrawled on the door in gold spray paint, "YOU MIGHT AS WELL LIVE."

"Mona, would you like me to run you a bath?"

She nodded slowly. On a good day Mona could sit in the bath for two hours, smoking and dreaming up her next spectacle. It didn't bother her that the communal tub was a century old and hadn't been cleaned in twenty years and that the walls were painted with hideous hippie graffiti—fairies and flowers and unicorns, mostly in lavender.

I ran her bath—extra hot—and walked her upstairs. She soaked for a long while, then put on some pajamas and allowed me and Pink to take her out for pizza and *Raising Arizona* at the neighborhood theater pub. By the next day she was healed—the imperious and condescending Mona we all knew and loved/hated was back.

This first meltdown shook me up good. But I soon understood it was nothing out of the ordinary, just the flipside of the creative process, the eviscerated emptiness following the birth. The trick to getting her through her post-partum shit was to put a notebook and pencil in her hands so she could start committing her hallucinations to paper. That and, of course, pot.

Money

It was my third day as a data entry temp for the City of Portland. I spent eight hours entering things like JX167HJ50 into the appropriate spaces of computerized spreadsheets. XC90FH23 <tab> <tab> 1/13/96 <tab> <tab> F2HU33M <tab> <tab> C66 <return>. For all I knew I was dropping bombs on North Korea and turning large tracts of prairie into Walmarts. It didn't feel like honest work in pursuit of beauty and truth, that's for sure. At least it was only a two-week assignment.

"Hey Jack! I just realized that as of today I have thirty-three years and six months until retirement!" hollered the three-hundred-pound brunette in the next cubicle.

"Oh yeah? I've got twenty-eight years, three months, and five days," countered Jack, the foxy gay office manager.

I resolved to become a stripper or kill myself, and whipped out a little notebook to start a list of pros and cons. Either choice presented a highroad compared to office whoring, that was clear.

I had had the best training in critical thinking our nation could provide and I couldn't come up with anything very critical of the sex industry. Degrading? Not compared to the brain-melting hamster cage

I was in at that moment. Exploitative? Of whom? In a free market situation, each party would enter into the business willingly and prices would be set by the laws of supply and demand. Human sexual appetites being what they were, the supply side stood to make a pretty sweet profit. If only the nice entitled liberal arts ladies could stop twisting their engagement rings long enough to consider who stood to profit most from sex economics, the patriarchy would crumble.

Stripping was the Little League of the sex industry. It represented a safe and not-so-invasive testing ground for my theories. As far as I could tell it was an honest exchange: a dollar for a smile. In fact it seemed to be one line of work in which society's entrenched misogyny was more or less absent. Guys worshipped strippers and totally prostrated themselves at the Altar of the Naked Woman. The women I had met were entrepreneurs. They made their own rules, set their own hours, and drew their own boundaries. There were no middlemen. The girls were free to embrace whatever far-out philosophies they wanted and could even proselytize from the stage. And they certainly weren't unwittingly selling arms to Third World nations. The worst that could be said about strippers was that they were flouting society's conventions.

A flunky came over with a fresh pile of numbers and letters to be typed into the computer, and I snapped out of my reverie. My adrenaline was pumping and my ego had swelled to Che Guevara proportions thinking about so much revolution. I took a walk to the pissoir to cool down. On the way I quietly clocked my fellow hamsters with my best sociologist stare. These kind, bland, fashionless people had swallowed the status quo hook, line, and sinker and Lord look how fat it'd made them! They were beached whales with little fire left in them. They'd given up on beauty and truth—perhaps they'd never even thought of it. Sure could count, though! Twenty-eight years, three months, and five days until big gay Jack could sit in his easy chair and channel surf without interruption.

I'd seen enough people who toed the line in my first five years to know that I wasn't one of them. Maybe I'd finally found my tribe. Strippers! Who disavowed the proverbial fig leaf and were unashamed of their bodies and their sexuality. Who found the key to the Garden of Eden and let themselves back in. Whose mere existence threatened polite society so much that it refused to even think about sex work, and instead made grand pronouncements of degradation and victimization in a fierce attempt to cast aspersions on any words of truth that might fall from a stripper's painted lips. Dangerous broads, man. Total menace to society. I was in.

* * *

I started spending a lot more time at the Magic Gardens. It was air conditioned and offered respite from the hot August sun, and Dave the English cook always fed us. And on Saturdays, Fat Jerry the bartender made us omelets, and we'd sit around listening to *Led Zeppelin IV* and drinking gimlets until the first yahoo came in.

The Saturday afternoon crowd was depressing as a rule. Old geezers who lived in the transient motels came in wearing all the clothing they had so as not to have it stolen. They'd sit at the rack sweating and offer a dollar every four songs. Jack would hobble in with his cane, dressed in a down parka. His thick glasses magnified his bugged-out eyes as he stared blankly and drooled. Black Larry would stop by—always in a spiffy suit—order Chivas and demand, "Show me the pink, baby," and "Spread it." The girls were inordinately nice to Black Larry because once upon a time he'd tipped very well. But since retirement he'd blown his cash. On them.

Black Larry liked me because I was a big-assed white girl. He was forever croaking licentious crap in my ear, which was uncomfortable and spitty because he'd had a tracheotomy. He had a serious chip on his shoulder and was probably the most racist person I'd ever met. He hated "niggers" and got really weird and schizo when non-whites came in. They were all lazy no-goods in his eyes. And Larry—"Black Larry"—was in fact black. He was so racist he'd get a stick up his ass if a gal so much as danced to James Brown or Jimi Hendrix. One time he gave Zyola, another curvy broad with a big white ass, half a dozen bottles of perfume, each with the word "white" in the name. White Shoulders. White Linen. White Whatever Else. One hundred and fifty bucks' worth. She knew because she returned them.

August melted into September and I was hurting for cash. I still wanted to be a stripper in theory, but was just a wee bit terrified to take the stage and drop my trousers. Mona was my stage mom.

"Watch and learn. Watch and learn."

So I did. I watched Sasha—a diminutive Irish sweet-tart who had an outsized attitude that more than clothed her when she was naked. "No greenery, no scenery!" she'd snarl in her hoarsey brogue. She had black hair cut in a shag—way before the shag's comeback—and wore suede cowboy boots she'd picked up at Goodwill. She danced to a lot of INXS.

I marveled at Rose, an older gal with chubby cheeks and wide, childlike eyes. She had a tattoo of a rose on her right shoulder. That and her head of dirty blonde pin curls were all you could see as she sat on the stage with her back to the room. Only when you looked at her reflection in the mirror did you notice that she was all but finger-banging herself, making naughty porno faces for the benefit of the completely-engrossed guy sitting at the rack behind her.

I watched Jenny, a tiny Asian chick with fake tits who wore white chaps and white leather stiletto thigh-high boots. She danced exclusively to heavy metal and somehow managed to do flips and cartwheels and other wacky gymnastics on the Magic's 5' × 8' stage. That's how tiny she was. She had a big husband, though, to carry her bags.

It was evident that there were as many styles of stripping as there were girls. What I found least moving were girls like Jenny who, from the moment they hit the stage, were a dance routine with fewer and fewer clothes. This seemed silly to me. What kind of sexuality is implied when a girl swings around a pole upside down or does gymnastics or a *Solid Gold* dance routine with no clothes on? To me stripping was not about dancing, it was about stripping—the act of disrobing. The girls who really got under my skin were seductresses who knew instinctively that the more you tease your prey, the sweeter the kill. The allure of the striptease wasn't so much the gynecological show as it was the slow unveiling of forbidden fruit. My absolute favorite naked ladies could keep you on the edge of your seat for an entire song by simply undoing a garter belt. Ladies like Mona.

* * *

Black Larry kept bugging me. When was I going to audition? I'd let him know, right?

I'd wink and say, "Any day, Larry, any day."

But the truth was I didn't know when or if I'd audition. I was scared, intimidated. Something told me that once you started, you couldn't go back, that stripping was an all-consuming lifestyle choice and not just a means of putting off the real world for a few months or years.

Mona, Pink, and I went to lots of clubs. Mo was the queen of scamming free drinks and steak dinners, so we three skinflint vagabonds lived pretty well for a while. We'd get up around ten o'clock, ease Mona through her treacherous morning existential crises, then drink coffee and smoke cigarettes at the hipster coffee shop, Umbra Penumbra, until our free ride presented himself. By two we'd have some poor Joey roped in, buying us fancy champagne cocktails and escargots at a swanky hotel bar or something. We'd ditch him and head to the Magic for the after-work regulars who were so desperate for relief from the humdrum that they were a guaranteed free meal. Probably pot, too.

My favorite hours were those spent at the strip clubs. Mona was respected by the other strippers. They'd all come by and say hi and soon I knew Sasha, Claudia, Morgan, June, Nikki, Tracy, Teresa, Rain, Venus, and more beyond the fake name basis.

"Watch and learn!" reminded Mona, knowing full well I'd take the plunge sooner or later.

If a really hot seventies song came on—say, Al Green or Marvin Gaye—she'd bounce off her barstool and slither gracefully around the joint, usually forcing me to join her, teaching me the Texas two-step along the way. Occasionally she'd oblige us all with an impromptu striptease, provided the working girls would cede the stage for a song or two. Seeing Mo strip out of her wool lumberjack jacket, Elmer Fudd hat, ratty cashmere sweater, patched blue jeans, clunky boots, and stinky socks (she always ceremoniously sniffed them, sitting catlike onstage) to reveal her superhero body—big tits, humongous bush, and bald head—was art incarnate. Certainly not a dry crotch in the house.

I felt so at home in these sleazy dive bars, the customers quickly becoming my trusted friends. Mo would point out moves she thought beyond disgusting. The rather standard hip grind, for instance, which she said "makes you look like you're taking a shit."

Mona's brand of striptease was psychological. It required getting into character—the vixen temptress—and never dropping it for a second.

She was all class, even when holding a stinky sock or pair of panties to her face and inhaling deeply. Even when hurling an ashtray at a cretinous customer's head. Even when collapsing in tears at the bar.

I started practicing moves in front of a mirror in my cramped studio apartment to a soundtrack of the Ramones, the Clash, David Bowie, and Marlene Dietrich. I picked through slips and robes at Goodwill and looked for underthings at Fantasy Video, which had lots of creepy eighties lingerie: dollar garters, peek-a-boo bras, crotchless panties. When I came across a pair of $55 "worn and refinished" seven-inch platform heels, covered in sparkly burgundy glass bits and three sizes too big for me, I knew it was time. I'd found my ruby slippers. I could click my heels three times, say "there's no place like home," and take it *off*.

What's in a Name, Part Two

"What's your name?"

"Viva."

"No, what's your *real* name?"

Answer:

a. annoyed silence

b. "That is my real name."

c. "Viva Las Vegas. My parents were big Elvis fans. My brother's name is Kid Creole."

d. "Viva in Norwegian."

e. "Ann."

f. All of the above, depending on how persistent the dumbass is.

Guys always want to know your real name, what you do outside of work, what's behind the glittering façade. And that's the one thing we don't let them see.

My given name, although I loved it, was unpronounceable to anyone outside of Norway. I definitely wanted a stripper name. And why not? It's fun to develop a new character, one you can summon up by merely changing your name. Right, Miss Monroe? Mr. Bowie? Monsieur Dylan?

I'd been mulling over the name thing for several weeks when mine struck me over coffee and a scone and a journal at Umbra Penumbra. I loved Warhol, sure, but the real reason I chose "Viva" was because it was my real name, transposed into Stripper. Since Andy's Viva did the one name thing, and because I was running with Teresa Dulce, Miss Mona Superhero, and Rain Stormm, I would need a surname. Viva... Viva... Las Vegas!

I'd never been to Vegas and never wanted to go. I joked that I was saving it for my wedding. It sounded tacky, cheap, and totally Walt Disney. I called it the capital of the postmodern world, devoted to cheap greed and classy trash and trashy class and overdone emptiness, an altar to capitalism and a study in paradoxes. Kind of like me—the overeducated highfalutin preacher's kid, stripping.

Audition

I woke up on the morning of September 30 with a steely resolve. I would audition.

It was my ex-boyfriend's birthday, the brown-eyed Libra boy I'd dated from age fourteen to nineteen. Truthfully, he was half the reason I'd been on the run the last three years, hopping from continent to continent, resolutely homeless. The bastard had broken my heart good, and if I was going to take the plunge and become a stripper, September 30 would have to be the day. It was a fuck-you to love, a disavowal of any sort of normal future with a decent husband and 2.5 children. In spite of my academic perspective and admiration of gals like Mona and Teresa, this was my idea of my new career: Fallen Woman—preacher's daughter thrown to the wolves in a dirty timber town. A descent into the dark side.

COME SEE
Miss Mona's
LADIES OF
LEISURE
CABARET

FEATURING

VIVA
LAS VEGAS

JUNE
29TH

BERBATI'S PAN • 231 SW ANKENY

I didn't have much of anything sexy or cute in my wardrobe after four years of college in the Berkshires. After much agonizing, I settled on the cream-colored satin and lace slip my mom bought me in high school to wear under some hideous dress she'd bribed me into for my semi-annual visit to Dad's flock. The look I was going for was shy innocence. I was the newbie, after all. Better to use my stage fright to my advantage. Plus, paired with the red rhinestone heels, the look was so wonderfully *Wizard of Oz*. All I needed was a small dog and my fall from grace would be complete.

I peeled off my street clothes in the Magic's shoebox-sized dressing room. Mona had helped me do my makeup at home, which was good because now my hands were shaking so badly I was having trouble working the buckle on my seven-inch ruby slippers. I slipped into my dress and panties, then gave myself a little pep talk in the mirror while Mona went to the bar to get me a drink. She poured a greyhound down my throat and sent me to the jukebox with a spanking. Tottering in my first pair of real heels, I punched in three songs: the Cowboy Junkies' lugubrious cover of "Sweet Jane" (a standard of my teenage romance), Dusty Springfield's "Son of a Preacherman" (for obvious reasons), and "Dazed and Confused" by Led Zeppelin ('cause I was, sort of).

And so I took the stage one Monday afternoon, a Midwestern tomboy gussied up to look like a baby doll with a fifteen-minute routine as loaded with symbolism as a goddamn wedding. Even the soundtrack I had chosen was so personally heartbreaking that the tears were quite literally ready-to-fall.

But the jukebox wrested control of my destiny. Motherfucker refused to play "Sweet Jane," so instead I got started off on the right foot, spinning around to the happy strains of "Son of a Preacherman," smiling and giggling. Thus I was born again with a cute, insolent, what-the-hell smirk that never left me all my stripper days, a smirk that let everyone know that I knew what was up and not to take this naked-chick thing so seriously.

I was coy and girlish to the cotton-candy soul of "Preacherman," using my Sunday slip to great effect. I raised the hem to just below my ass and moved the fabric back and forth flirtatiously, shyly biting my lip like a naughty two-year-old. Then, slipping out of the loose straps to reveal my little breasts, I put my hand to my mouth and feigned surprise, just like I'd seen in off-color comics from the fifties, wherein ladies' panties "accidentally" fall down while they're holding two bags of groceries.

The sweet Motown-like strains of the Dusty Springfield song seemed to naturally summon this strange flirtatious creature I'd never met. But when "Dazed and Confused" came on the jukebox and I started writhing on the floor nearly nude, no one was more surprised than I was. I'd always blossomed onstage and was adept at reading what people wanted, but this was nuts! Sure there were only five guys at the bar that Monday afternoon, but their eyes were wide and their mouths half open. Taking this as a sign that my audition was going reasonably well, I slipped out of my skivvies. Sliding the white lace panties down my hips was like diving into a pool: awfully scary to contemplate, but once you're in, there's no turning back. I was and would forever be a stripper.

Finally I had succumbed to a sisterhood. It was refreshing and exciting. After years of running with the boys in rebellion, I got to learn how to be a girl. Soon I'd be shopping for lingerie and makeup, and a habitué of costume stores, magic shops, and wig salons. Most refreshing and exciting of all, I had wrested control of my morality from the claws of social indoctrination. I was *free*. And I'd made forty bucks in two songs!

Dave the English cookie took me back into the kitchen, photocopied my ID, explained the rules (no drugs except for pot), and had me sign a waiver with my real name and my stripper name—Viva Las Vegas.

Back in my blue jeans with a bit of extra cash, I took everyone out for drinks. I was ecstatic, positively vibrating with excitement. The whole world seemed to have cracked open like an oyster for me to suck on—salty, sweet, and sexy as hell. Glitter, eyeliner, hair dye, wigs, false eyelashes, high heels, G-strings, pasties, feather boas, Otis Redding, table dances, the economics of desire and the philosophies of the fringe, the heart of the cowgirl nation and the quiet of 3 AM.

How to Strip, Part One

1. Wear layers. The more you've got on, the more you get to peel off.

2. It's the peeling that's the titillating part. Take your time. Slow the fuck down. Let the curve of your back become a religious experience.

3. For heaven's sake, don't dance to Natalie Merchant. Pick something that moves you, but be sensitive to the desires of your audience. I've known girls who strip to the Eagles' "Hotel California" out of sheer generosity. That's a bit much. But Rage Against the Machine isn't always appropriate. Think Marvin Gaye, *Super Hits of the '70s* or AC/DC. White guys of any age or level of hip love the Rolling Stones. Many really love country. Black guys aren't that common in Portland, but I know from a strip in NYC that they don't think much of the New York Dolls.

4. Smile smile smile. You could be wearing clamdiggers and a parka for your entire set, and the guy you're smiling at will keep offering up his paycheck in one-dollar increments. Make him think you like him. That's why he's there.

5. Ditto eye contact. More effective than a boob job for augmenting your tips.

6. A boob job doesn't really augment your tips at all. For some it augments their confidence and *hence* their earnings.

7. Be really nice to the girl(s) you're working with.

8. Be even nicer to the management.

9. *Hard-to-get* makes more money than *easy*. StripTEASE! StripTEASE!

   For example: Say you've got on a long-sleeved button-up yellow fuzzy sweater, short white skirt, white cotton bra and panties. What's the sexiest part? The buttons! Unbuttoning the top should take a whole song. A bra should always be worn. What kind of girl doesn't wear a bra? Short skirts that make you look like a schoolgirl are always sexier than those expensive gold lamé and rhinestone Vegas gowns. White cotton panties are almost always sexier than a G-string that leaves nothing to the imagination. Remember that men are visual, imaginative creatures. And that everybody loves a challenge.

10. You've got a great job. If you pretend you really enjoy it, you start to really enjoy it. Your enjoyment will be infectious, and every dick in the bar will feel he's just set foot in paradise. Revere the power of positive thinking. It manifests as money.
11. Always say thank you. Even if it's just a buck. If it's food stamps or metro passes or coins, nicely tell 'em to go fuck themselves.
12. Never underestimate your customer. The guy in the t-shirt, khakis, and Chuck Taylors might be a millionaire. Then again, most millionaires are pretty tight.

Candy

It was a trial by fire. I didn't even have time to get nervous.

Jerry called me at 5 PM. A girl had cancelled and could I cover her Saturday closing shift?

"Are you crazy? I just auditioned! I've never stripped before! I can't do a SATURDAY NIGHT!"

"Of course you can, Viva."

"You're nuts!"

"So you'll be here at eight thirty?"

Pause. "Okay. Whatever. But you're crazy!"

Holy fuck. I ran next door to tell Mona but she was out. I grabbed my toiletries and got in line for the Lawn's communal shower. I shaved my legs and armpits and manicured my crotch. Then I threw the few things I'd assembled into an old duffel bag: a black zippered jumpsuit, a silver spangly disco ball dress, a ratty old Loverboy concert t-shirt that had Joan Jett on the back (so I wore it backwards), full-butt boy undies with "BABE" emblazoned on them and that old Sunday slip from high school. I raided Mona's stripper bag, too, grabbing a black velvet dress with feathers at the hem and her black vinyl platform superhero boots.

All I had to do to summon my inner rock star was to zip up those boots and *voila!* They were only two sizes too big and so a better choice than my size ten ruby slippers, which must have heeled some classy-ass drag queen in a past life.

I left notes on Mo's and Pink's doors, then hopped on my bicycle with my enormous bag and rode down to the Magic, cursing aloud all the way. I was scared shitless.

I walked my bike inside the bar and put it in the cold hallway separating the Magic from the top-secret Chinese gambling parlor next door. In the dressing room I met my co-worker, Candy—a tiny, ultra-tan, ultra-blonde, eighties-throwback mother of three. I chattered nervously that it was my first night, and she warmed up to me.

"You'll do fine, hon."

I dug through my tiny make-up bag—a relic from eighth grade— and put on some ten-year-old Coty powder, a thick line of black eyeliner, old Almay mascara, and a coat of "Vixen"-colored Revlon lipstick—the kind that stays on forever, no matter how many shirts you pull over your head. I slid into the BABE panties, a short white skirt, and a nubby, black cropped sweater. I looked at myself in the mirror. What was I doing? I wasn't a stripper! I was a scruffy, dirty-blonde tomboy with strong shoulders, tiny tits, and wide hips. My legs were long and well-muscled, however, and my skin was creamy white, young and glowing.

"Fuck this, I can strip." I gave myself another pep talk. "Sure, lots of guys will prefer Candy, with her hard fake tits and weathered face, but everyone's different. And I look fuckin' hot naked."

The whiskey was obviously taking effect. And I did look hot naked. I'd been at war with my body since puberty hit, but even in the dark post-eating-disorder days when my metabolism was totally screwed up and my weight shot up to one hundred fifty-five pounds I thought I looked much better naked than clothed. My athletic build and slender waist and curvy hips looked awesome *au naturel*, but, I thought, heavy with clothes on. Still I'd have traded anything to be a sickly-looking size one....

Whatever! Candy was on her third song doing wacky acrobatics in a G-string. I would be quite a contrast. She was dancing to hair metal, Mötley Crüe and stuff. So I plugged in "Soldier Boy"—cute, sixties, innocent—then Bowie's "Rebel, Rebel." Then, hands shaking, holding a whiskey on the rocks, the Supremes' "Baby, Baby, Where Did Our Love Go?"

I wanted to cry. Wanted to quit. I hadn't even started! The rack was full of men I'd never seen during my brief tenure as a Magic barfly. But when the first bright notes of "Soldier Boy" echoed through the room, I slipped all of a sudden into performance mode and walked self-assuredly to the stage. One thing you must be when stripping is confident. If you don't feel confident, you must fake it. If you don't fake it, the stage magic won't work, and the men will treat you like a dog.

I milked the shy, coy newbie trick for all it was worth. I noticed right away that guys responded well to the innocent, giggly stripper shtick and stuck with it most of the night. Occasionally I'd try the sultry vixen on for size, imitating Mona some, but it never went over as well as the smile/laugh/thank you!

The boys were extremely complimentary. I figured they were just trying to make me comfortable.

"I'm new. This is my first night," I'd say over and over, trying to excuse whatever wasn't up to snuff.

"Well, ya sure can't tell."

"You're a natural."

"When do you work again?"

Many of them were whispering about my ass. At first I tried to block them out so as not to start crying or yelling at them. Then I realized every time I turned around and displayed it in all its glory they'd put down another dollar. Maybe a five. My butt stole the show. I had loathed it ever since I'd sprouted hips in sixth grade, and these freaks were absolutely gaga over it! I couldn't believe it. Didn't they read *Cosmo?*

The night passed slowly. I felt incredibly awkward much of the time, but the audience was so encouraging that I managed to maintain my stage presence. When I got too nervous I made small talk, and was delighted when I found common ground with the guy who spoke German, the fellow wearing the "Ely, Minnesota" t-shirt, the gentleman who went to Amherst College.

Somehow I made it through the five-hour shift. I was so exhausted by the end that it was hard to count my tips and calculate the ten percent tip-out. I gave twenty-five bucks to Terri—the elderly night-time bartender—and pocketed two hundred. I felt like a millionaire. I'd barely come up with my hundred-and-seventy-five-dollar rent that month and now I had TWO HUNDRED DOLLARS.

I couldn't wait to bike home, see Mo and Pink, and go to bed. They called the Magic to congratulate me. I said I'd be home in ten minutes. Then Candy came into the dressing room.

"Let's go dancing!"

"What? We just got done dancing."

"Come on! It's fun! You have to."

"It's 2:30 AM. Don't the bars close? I'm so tired."

"It's an all-ages dance club. I'll call us a cab."

Strippers are REALLY GOOD at getting what they want. Obviously she'd had some blow or something. I was dead tired and a little delirious; my back felt like it was broken. I'd given so much of myself —performed like I'd never performed before, pulled every hat trick I knew, from politics to Shakespeare to Midwestern folk legends to contemporary art. But what the hell. When was I gonna get to ride with a chick like Candy again? Didn't I have some obligation to her, me being so new and dorky and working her money shift? Didn't my devotion to beauty and truth and journaling at the coffee shop require me to go adventuring when the opportunity presented itself?

So I went. We took a cab to her apartment on SW Broadway. It was only twenty blocks away, but during the time it took us to get there she told me her life story, and it was the stereotypical stripper stuff: step-dad abused her, ex-boyfriend abused her, three kids, her sister taking care of them, some drugs but not as much as before, etc., etc. And did I like girls?

We took an elevator to the third floor and tiptoed over her children and sister—all sleeping on the floor. Candy needed to get ready to go dancing. I couldn't believe I was in this darkened room filled with sleeping babies waiting for an over-the-hill stripper stereotype to finish snorting coke so she could squire me to an all-ages dance venue at three in the morning. Ah, the life of the mind!

My patience was wearing thin. Finally I had her call me a cab. I was exhausted. I had friends waiting for me. I left Candy to her wacky life. I never saw her again.

Thank You for Supporting the Arts

While "stereotypical strippers" like Candy do exist, they are the exception, not the rule. Besides being a cokehead and an inattentive single mother, the stereotypical stripper has been sexually abused, is an addict, is uneducated, has few options, prostitutes herself on the side, and unequivocally needs saving. Thank God Portland is a place where if you give voice to such opinions, you are considered the kind of bigot who thinks blacks shouldn't vote and Hitler was right. It's not that Portlanders are so enlightened; largely it has to do with Oregon's Constitution.

Dating to 1857, the state's Constitution provides the broadest protection of free speech in the nation. In Article 1, Section 8, it states: "No law shall be passed restraining the free expression of opinion, or restricting the right to speak, write, or print freely on any subject whatever." Oregon's Supreme Court takes this directive very seriously, and the occasional attempts to zone or otherwise regulate strip clubs out of existence have always been struck down. Add to this basic capitalism (beer + naked chicks = $$$), and you've got the highest number of strip clubs per capita in the world.

Oregon's sheer number of clubs, in addition to their visibility, normalizes what goes on within them. In Portland, meeting a stripper is as common as meeting a barista, and patronizing a strip club is as normal as going to a rock club. Few strip clubs charge a cover to enter, and drink prices are on par with other bars in town. This allows for a varied audience, and young artists, students, and musicians fill the seats as often as solo guys and bachelor parties, and women make up a significant part of the clientele. The interaction between dancer and customer is seen not so much as titillating as *entertaining*, and taking your clothes off for money is not considered unusual.

Strippers here appreciate that basic respect they're afforded, and although they make considerably less money than girls in big fancy Houston/ Florida/ NYC clubs, working conditions in Portland are better and we don't pay the exorbitant stage fees common elsewhere. (Although paid a wage until the early nineties, strippers nationwide work for tips only, and often have to pay to take the stage to the tune of fifty to three hundred dollars.) Most clubs in Portland charge no stage fees at all, requiring only that the dancer tip out the bar staff.

Our customers couldn't be more normal, either. In fact, the relationship between the customers and the performer is bizarrely Victorian. Guys are uncommonly polite at Portland strip clubs, generally speaking. They say please and thank you, rarely hit on you (unless they're young and dumb), and rarely even say anything off-color. Most of the time they try to make eye contact rather than stare at those parts that are normally covered. Touching, of course, is strictly prohibited. Compare this to a night out at a regular bar, where guys will grab your ass, say stupid shit, and expect you to lie down if they buy you a drink.

I found this interaction around "sex" wonderfully refreshing. Being a shy girl who giggles a lot and has an apple ass, I got harassed more in high school and college by professors, teachers, and men on trains than I ever would at strip clubs. It was a huge relief to feel untouchable on-stage. And I was in charge. I permitted the audience's gaze; it wasn't foisted on me like it would be on the street, in a classroom, or at a bar.

And was stripping even about sex? Nine times out of ten, for the stripper it's about performance, especially in Portland, where good old-fashioned burlesque never went out of vogue. No doubt the men come in for a frisson of sexual excitement, but men will visit their favorite foxy bartender for the same reason. All you really have to do is smile at them and they get all fired up. Ultimately, stripping is no more about sex than Botticelli's "Venus" or modern dance. It is performance and, to my mind, art.

When I walked into my first strip club, I'd been studying art for years. I'd worked at an art museum throughout college and had been to hundreds of operas, plays, and dance performances. Immediately I felt that watching a girl move her body on stage, communing with her audience, subversively naked, was the best art of my time. This was the end of the century, the end of the millennium, and every artist seemed to be making self-conscious, self-referential, solipsistic shit that a person would need a PhD to comprehend (that or all-out kitsch, which to my palette was even worse). Naked Girl Art spoke to everyone, across racial, ethnic, and class divides. And you couldn't deny it was real; it all but stank of humanity.

Which is how, midway through my first shell-shocked shift and already sick to death of saying "thank you" one hundred and fifty times an hour, sick even of *merci, danke,* and *asante sana,* I came up with my signature line. A battle cry, a *raison d'être* that I've mewed jubilantly at least one million times since: *Thank you, ladies and gentlemen, for supporting the arts!*

Born Blonde

A stripping hangover, for me, anyway, is always a kind of sweet exhaustion. I wake up around eight thirty and loll in bed for a while, every limb throbbing in pain. It's never an alcohol hangover as I rarely get drunk, especially off the thimbleful of booze that is commonly poured in strippers' drinks, but an exhaustion resultant from the cumulative effects of giving my everything nonstop for five hours. It feels good; it's something I'm proud of. I'm a great master of ceremonies and maybe even a great stripper. In any case I get better and better at just being me every day. Plus I have a pile of cash to show for my all-nude night and nowhere to be until the next day or the day after. Usually I go to the coffee shop and write about it for a few hours. Then I have a drink. Stripping is so lovely.

After my debut alongside cokehead Candy, I slept the sleep of the dead for four hours. I awoke ecstatic. I did it! I was a stripper!

I lolled in bed extra long, then rousted Mona and Pink and marched them through Junkie Park, trading catcalls with bums, to the Gypsy Tavern for a Bloody Mary brunch. They were proud of me, too, and enjoyed my childlike elation. I had blueberry pancakes. Pink had eggs. Mona, of course, had the chicken-fried steak.

On our way home we stopped at Fred Meyer to buy some Born Blonde hair bleach. I'd been a Born Blonde my junior and senior years at rich kid college, hitting the bottle in places as far flung as Tanzania and Bali. But, in an attempt at maturity, I'd finally grown it all out to a dirty-blonde shag. It was very unremarkable and not at all ¡*Viva!*

Back at the Lawn Pink spread on the bleach and then we all played old Atari games he'd salvaged from the trash. An hour later my hair was Born Blonde and my transformation complete. Here at last was Viva Las Vegas—a blonde giggly ringer for Marilyn Monroe, a big-butted, smart-assed smirker extraordinaire, a rock 'n' roll animal, a honky-tonk angel.

Heaven

My first scheduled shift was Tuesday noon to four. After the Saturday night shift, I felt like an old pro and didn't find it necessary to apologize to Heaven, the other dancer, for half the shift.

The day shift at the Magic was always slow and pathetic. The bar tipped you twenty bucks just for showing up by eleven thirty and often-times even bought your first drink. The lunch crowd arrived promptly at noon and ate their steak & eggs and fish & chips right at the rack. Gross. Once they'd gone, customers were few and far between. Bums fresh off the Greyhound or out of the clink would talk your ear off over a two-dollar Coors Light. Jack and Black Larry would make their rounds. Sleazy lawyers stopped in for an afternoon table dance. Lawyers were always the worst. They seemed to feel they could get away with murder. Probably could. At the Magic they were constantly getting tossed for taking out their erect cocks.

Heaven was beautiful in a fallen investment banker sorta way: long, lithe, and tan with a smart light-brown bob and haughty, aristocratic features that matched her haughty, aristocratic attitude. I didn't even try to make small talk with her, just danced my three songs, retreated to the dressing room to change, then sucked on a vodka soda at the bar while she finished her set.

Around three in the afternoon a suit came in. He was with Channel 8 evening news. They were doing a little spot on an upcoming vote regarding zoning ordinances. Yuppies in Portland annually try to up-

SEEK YOUR SALVATION AT

The

MAGIC GARDEN

FULL LIQUOR BAR ★ DAILY LUNCH SPECIAL ★ KITCHEN OPEN 'TIL 2AM

OPEN DAILY 12 NOON TO 2 AM ★ OPEN SUNDAY AT 6PM

MISS MOMAS

VIXENS *of* VOODOO *Cabaret*

FEB **9**TH DOORS OPEN AT 6PM SHOW

STARTS 8PM LATE SHOW 11:30

end Oregon's ultra-liberal constitutional protections of free speech. And every year, God bless it, they fail. Channel 8 wanted an industry spokesperson to give a little soundbite.

I got very excited. The revolutionary chicks I ran with were primed and ready to give everyone an earful.

"Call Teresa! Call Teresa!" I chirped.

"We don't have time for someone to come down here. One of you will have to do it."

Heaven stuck her head out of the dressing room. "It's not going to be me!"

"Why not?" I begged her. "You gonna run for president or something?"

"Yes."

That left me. The newbie. Having to speak for and defend the honor of one of the biggest stripping communities in the world. Well, why not?

The film crew shot me slowly, sensually dancing to the Portishead song "Sour Times." I wore my black jumpsuit and looked pretty striking for the scruffy puppy that I was, with my platinum blonde hair and bloodred lips.

I toyed with my long zipper. They liked that and got a close-up. *Ziiiiiip.* One more time. *Ziiiiiip.* Again, with feeling! *Ziiiiiiiip.*

The newsboys hung around to get their soundbite while I slipped into my glamorous street clothes: old Levi's 501s, black motorcycle boots, a grungy white thermal, and my uncle's old army t-shirt. They sat me on a barstool and made sure any customers were out of sight. Lisa poured me a shot. The suit stuck a microphone in my face and asked me a few questions about the zoning ordinances up for vote. I knew next to nothing about it but had a lot to say about my new cause. Naked Ladies Are Alright! Are Art! Should Be Cherished or Left Alone! You could practically hear the drum rolls, the fifes and horns in the background as I waxed patriotic, singing, "Naked bodies are beautiful, are gorgeous. There's nothing wrong with them. And America is a country that values and protects free speech. If I wanna dance around naked, it is my right to do so."

My adrenaline was pumping hard as the suits shook my hand, packed up, and left. I downed another shot, mounted my bike, and headed up Couch Street, a brazen conqueror high on victory and whiskey. Back at the Lawn, I scrounged around for a half-blank videotape on which to record my folly for posterity and, at ten o'clock, a bunch of us gathered around to watch the news.

There I was. "Viva." Slinky onstage and cocksure in front of the camera, talking about beauty, truth, America, art. Mona was so proud. Pink was laughing. Teresa called and offered her congratulations.

Yessiree, this stripping thing fit like a glove. And the beautiful idea of Heaven for president has never left me.

Mom, I'm a Stripper

It was a brisk morning in mid-October, just before eight, when I set out for a run. Just because I'd been out 'til 3 AM drinking and dancing didn't mean I could skip the morning routine that I'd kept since age twelve.

My running route took me through my favorite parts of Northwest Portland. It wasn't the safest route—dappled with belligerent drunks and homeless encampments—but I'm a fast runner and nearly everyone I encountered was incapacitated anyway. I loved running down 16th Avenue to Thurman Street, under the enormous ribs of the Fremont Bridge. The concrete columns made a cathedral out of the gritty industrial space underneath them, the on-ramps soaring through the sky, gracefully curving to meet at the main span of the bridge. It reminded me of a woman's nether-lands. It also reminded me of my mom. Mom loved bridges and engineering, and I looked forward to the day I could give her a tour of my new town. I ran under the bridge, over the railroad tracks, and down Front Avenue, where I'd catch colorful glimpses of the gigantic ships moored alongside the old grain elevators that fringed the Willamette River. At 9th Avenue I'd turn back towards home, passing the mounted police stables, then heading west under the Lovejoy Bridge. The Lovejoy's on-ramp effectively bisected Northwest Portland's industrial district. To the south, towards downtown, were a handful of artists' lofts and a thriving population of pushers and prostitutes. To the north was no man's land. I like no man's lands. But I'm a fast runner.

Back at the Lawn I slipped into my kimono and grabbed my shower things. Fortunately I only had to wait for one person to finish using the shower all forty tenants shared. Then I pulled on my black velvet leggings, motorcycle boots, and pink wool turtleneck and bicycled down to Umbra Penumbra to meet Anne Johanson.

Anne was something of a legend in my hometown. Eight years my senior, she'd spent a year in Russia and then attended the University of Chicago. She was artistic, smart, and eccentric, and I was flattered whenever people likened me to her. I was even more flattered when she called to say she'd be passing through Portland, and asked if I'd like to join her for coffee.

She was already at the coffee shop when I arrived. I was overjoyed to see a familiar face from Minnesota. Anne was on a road trip, visiting friends in California and Colorado. She talked for a while about her travels before cutting to the chase.

"So, Eric tells me you're now an erotic dancer."

I blushed. Eric was my high school sweetheart's brother. He was working in Portland and kept his furniture at my apartment in exchange for the opportunity to occasionally crash on the futon. I hadn't told him not to tell anyone about my new career, but it hadn't occurred to me that he might actually spill the beans.

"Stripper, actually, is the term I prefer. Yes, I am. And I love it. I love it so much. I'm happier than I've ever been."

"Yeah, Eric mentioned something to that effect, too. Good for you. Do your parents know?"

"No way. I don't think they could handle it. And I'm not ready for them to rain on my parade."

"What do you think your dad will say?"

"Exactly. My dad can never find out. Ever."

Suddenly it occurred to me that if Eric had told Anne that I was a stripper, it wouldn't be long before the entire town of Grand Marais knew. Its population was well under 2000; gossip of this nature would travel like wildfire. The preacher's daughter is a stripper! I could just imagine the shitstorm that would kick up at the Bluewater Café, at Sven and Ole's Pizza, at Johnson's Big Dollar Grocery. And if Eric and Anne were talking about me stripping, there was a good chance that Mallory knew, too. As much as I loved and admired her, my ex-boyfriend's stepmother Mallory was one of the biggest gossips in town. And she was prominent in the Catholic Church, which was gossip central.

I approached the topic cautiously. "Have you told anyone up there about me being a stripper? Not that it really matters, but…"

"The only person I've talked about it with is Mallory. Mal adores you and is open-minded about everything. She thinks it's a hoot."

Fuck! *Mallory knew!* I blanched as white as my napkin. If Mal knew, all of Grand Marais knew. If all of Grand Marais knew, it was only a matter of time before my parents found out about my delinquency through the grapevine, even though they lived two hours away in Duluth.

I pretended not to let Anne's revelation faze me. It was so good to see her. There was no sense in ruining our coffee date by having a nervous breakdown. That I could do later in private.

* * *

"Hey, Mom, it's your daughter."

"Oh hi, honey! How are you?"

"I'm good. Guess who I just had coffee with? Anne Johanson."

"Oh how nice. I heard she's heading back to Chicago for law school."

"I don't know; we didn't really talk about that. Um… Mom? It's occurred to me that I need to tell you something important." Fuck. This wasn't going to be easy.

"What." Her tone changed dramatically; suddenly it was harboring a nuclear arsenal.

"Promise not to get upset. Promise! I don't have AIDS. I'm not pregnant. I think I might even still be a virgin…"

"Well, that's good. So what is it? Spit it out."

"Okay. Well…remember how we talked a lot about sex work this summer?"

We had talked a lot about sex work over the summer. I'd taken a sociology seminar senior year and come away very frustrated with academia's read on the sex industry. Mom and I spent long hours discussing it as we walked along Lake Superior, and she seemed pretty open-minded about my pro-sex-work opinions.

"Well… I'm not really a cocktail waitress. But I'm not a prostitute either! I'm a stripper. Don't be mad! Please don't be mad. I love it so much. I've never been happier."

"Oh GOD! Are you kidding me? With all of your talents, this is what you choose to do? A STRIPPER? What do you think your father is going to say about this?"

"Mom, *please* don't tell him. Please, please, please. He doesn't need to know."

"Well, I don't really want to ruin his life, so I won't tell him. But you better think twice about how what you're doing affects your family. Jesus! What about your brothers?"

What an absurd thing to say, I thought. What about my brothers? Were they branded with a scarlet letter because their sister was a stripper? "Okay, Mom, I'm going to get off the phone. I just want you to know that I'm safe and I'm happy. I'll call you next weekend. I love you."

"Bye," she spat as she hung up.

At least that was over with. And maybe she had a point. Maybe I should feel some tiny bit of remorse about my decision to strip and how it affected others. But then again, maybe it was my own fucking life to fuck up as I pleased. It's not like my parents never made any mistakes on their way to adulthood. Wasn't I allowed a few youthful indiscretions? Couldn't I "follow my bliss"—like they'd advised—for one fucking minute?

I went next door to see Pink. "I just told my mom I'm a stripper."

"Yeah? How'd that go?"

"I think I'd like to have a drink."

"Okay. Where? You name it."

"Let's go to Scandals. Gay bars always cheer me up."

One Cape Cod later I felt significantly better. In fact, I felt relieved. I didn't want to keep secrets from my parents; I loved and respected them too much. Well, that's not entirely true. I really wanted to keep this particular secret from my father for as long as possible. The fire and brimstone that was sure to rain from heaven when he found out would burn me alive. And I didn't want to be burned alive; I was having far too much fun.

How to Strip, Part Two

The Table Dance

First off, THREE RULES:

1. NO TOUCHING
    Rule #1 is often discreetly flouted. However, touching the customer when you are naked, even if you lose your footing and bump his knee, is technically prostitution.
2. NO TOUCHING YOUR NIPPLES, VAGINA, OR ASSHOLE
    Legally this is defined as masturbation and is impermissible by law. Rule #2 is almost always overlooked. Still, it's best to be subtle about it.
3. NO "DEALS"
    This varies from club to club. Indeed, some clubs advertise table dance specials. But if you give a guy two-for-one table dances at the Magic, the guy will want the same from every other girl and the girls will be pissed. At you.

How to Table Dance

Soliciting table dances is frowned upon downtown, if *de rigueur* in the 'burbs. Generally a gentleman will approach a dancer and inquire about a dance. Explain that dances are all-nude private dances, that touching is strictly forbidden, and that they cost twenty dollars a song. If he's into this type of usury, take him to the corner and unceremoniously remove all your clothes. Position yourself several feet away from the customer and, when the song begins, move around. When the song ends, unceremoniously get dressed and take the guy's money.

* * *

Table dances were a rare occurrence at the Magic. I'd seen only a couple of gals perform them, and they weren't the gals I ran with. Mona crinkled her little nose at the mention of them. I wouldn't form an opinion on them one way or another without having done one first, but I dreaded the day I'd be asked.

One extremely dead afternoon around two o'clock, after it'd become clear I wasn't going to leave work with more than forty bucks, a middle-aged gentleman, balding and with little round glasses, approached me in his wheelchair.

"How much for a dance?" he asked dully.

"It's twenty dollars a song, sir." I smiled apologetically, hoping he'd think the price far too expensive. After all, the song he paid for could easily be a two-minute Ramones song or, worse, anything by Elvis. All Elvis songs clock in under two minutes.

"I'd like two."

Shit! I inhaled quickly and shot an imploring look at Lisa, the weekday bartender, in hopes she'd save me. She just smiled and winked. I swallowed hard and made my way resolutely to the corner, gritting my teeth and cursing under my breath. The wheelchair guy followed close behind.

Magic's table dance area was in the cramped corner near the dressing room. There was an actual table there, set with a candle and a chair. I moved the chair out of the way so my customer could wedge his wheelchair into the tiny space. The other stripper had just plugged her songs into the jukebox and was heading for the stage. I silently prayed for two short songs, but to no avail. When the organ from Led Zeppelin's nearly five-minute opus "Your Time Is Gonna Come" droned out of the speakers, I felt like the whole bar was conspiring against me.

"Oooo, I just luuuv Led Zeppelin, don't you?" I purred, pulling off my little white baby doll slip.

The man didn't say anything, just stared at my naked breasts. I slowly began to dance, making absolutely sure I was three feet away, first facing him and then facing the stage, where I made a grimace at the other dancer. I could tell already that I didn't like table dancing, and if I made it through these two I vowed never to do one again. It was most definitely not the reason I'd become a stripper—to have guys hungrily eye my breasts and butt but miss the rest of the package. Nuh-uh! I was a performer. I needed a stage, lights, and an audience. This one-on-one crap felt falsely intimate. What the hell song was my co-worker going to torture me with next? Pink Floyd? The Doors' "The End"?

It was Blondie. "Tide is High." Long, but at least it was coy. I opted for small talk to see me through.

"So, what brings you to this bad neighborhood?" I asked sweetly.

"Lunch break," he said curtly.

"Gosh, is it lunchtime already?"

I didn't know what else to say. I really like your wheelchair? I just love bald men? I turned my back to him and let him project his fantasies on the wide white screen of my ass. The mariachi-style horns of the tune cheered me only a little. Normally I sang along with every Blondie song, but not this time. I felt too compromised, and I didn't want to drag Debbie Harry down with me.

Finally the song ended. The customer handed me a single folded bill, thanked me, and rolled out the door.

"Buh-bye!" I chirped after him. "Come again!"

Why had he only given me a single bill? He stiffed me. I knew it. Probably I deserved it; probably I'd performed the most uninspired table dance ever witnessed. Or maybe the guy was just a cheap bastard. When I finally unfolded the money in my hand I was floored.

"A fifty dollar bill! Holy moly! I've never even seen one of these before!"

Lisa grinned. "Wow, Viva! You gonna buy the bar a round?" With the exception of Lisa, myself, the other stripper and the cook, the bar was deserted.

"I just didn't think he really liked me," I said.

"Oh give me a break, Viva. Why would he buy a dance if he didn't like you?"

The next day I got up early, had coffee on 23rd Avenue and then bicycled to Cinema 21—an independent theater that showed lots of art films. They were having their annual poster sale and I was eager to get some art for my walls. The lobby of the theater was lined with huge garbage cans, each filled with rolled up posters. Most advertised Japanese gangster films, animation festivals, and gay/Jewish/Iranian films, and sold for anywhere between twenty and four hundred dollars. I was surprised that old movie posters were so expensive, but I browsed anyway.

Then I struck gold. An immaculate poster from *El Mariachi* by Robert Rodriguez. On it was a denim-clad man, shot from the waist down, carrying a guitar case and a machine gun and walking down the yellow centerlines of a desert highway. A large turtle crossed in the foreground.

The image was sacred to me. I'd found a much smaller version of it in a magazine sophomore year of college and it had steered me through that yuppie hell, reminding me who I thought I was: a fighter, a loner, a rebel who loved the open road, music and, uh, guns and turtles.

I had to have the poster. I held my breath as I looked at the price sheet on the wall.

EL MARIACHI: $50

I didn't have fifty bucks to spend on a poster. I barely made rent every month. But hadn't I just made fifty bucks in eight minutes the day before? I felt the thrill of the kill as I reached into the right pocket of my jeans where the fifty was, still folded. The poster would be mine.

I paid the film geek in charge of the moneybox and walked my new treasure down 21st Avenue to the framing shop on the corner of Flanders Street. I couldn't afford to have it framed, but for twenty bucks the guy would put it on poster board for me and attach hardware for hanging. Done! The poster would be ready in two hours.

I walked back to the Lawn beaming, thinking that maybe I should give table dancing just one more try. Sure it was ludicrous that a man would pay twenty dollars to look at my privates privately for one song, but I just spent fifty on a movie poster! And though something about table dancing made me queasy, like I was compromising my message of beauty and truth, the *El Mariachi* poster—its image my touchstone in college—represented freedom. And that balding fellow in the wheelchair had bought it for me in exchange for an up-close and personal look at my fabulous ass. Freedom.

Ring of Fire

For a while Mona, Pink, and I were inseparable. We were the Three Musketeers, broke as a joke but living for adventure and off of plunder and booty. I burned pretty hot on my own, but with these two pirates by my side we were an absolute conflagration.

It's good to be on fire. All ya gotta do is burn. Some people wait their entire lives and never get to experience it, so don't go about doing it half-assed. Don't worry about the inevitable burnout. Don't worry about anything at all. Just burn, baby, burn.

Mr. Pink was a trusty block of good dry wood. He was whipsmart and misanthropic to the extreme, the perfect foil for Mona's grandiosity and my naïveté. He was filled with sarcastic *bons mots*, had a cozy shoulder to cry on, and never let his life be upended by something so pedestrian as love. He was a solid block of good dry wood, very predictable and instrumental in a fire.

Every morning we'd waken to the promise of glorious new misadventures on the scuzzy streets of Portland. Not even brutal hangovers could keep us in bed; by eleven o'clock we'd be up and dressed. We'd decide where to go for breakfast, then let the wind blow our wildfire where it would.

A typical day found us meandering down Burnside to Umbra Penumbra for coffee and cigarettes. The ladies at the coffee shop always glowered at us as we burst through the door. As irresistible as I found Mona, many people hated her, especially women. I figured they were all just jealous.

We'd get big cups of coffee and grab a few magazines from Umbra's selection of zines, art mags, and alternative weeklies. Pink flipped through *Juxtaposed* and a weird Japanese catalog while Mona creamed her jeans over an old *Love and Rockets* comic and some guy's carefully cataloged photographs of a month's worth of bowel movements.

A man in a nice suit eyed us from the next table. Mona recognized him and choreographed an ambush; he'd make a fine date for the afternoon. Soon we'd conned him into taking us all to an early movie. That would give Pink enough time to get to work at Sin City by two o'clock.

Sin City was our new favorite haunt. An old-fashioned sex arcade that was open twenty-four hours a day, 365 days a year, it coincidentally shared a name with our favorite comic book.

Pink had been working the swing shift there for a couple of weeks to supplement his unemployment check. He manned the front counter where he could keep an eye on the merchandise. Condoms in every flavor and color lined the inside of the glass case alongside boxes of NO$_2$ cartridges; little pocket vibrators and bottles of pills touting natural aphrodisiac effects rubbed up against lubes, penis pumps, and the cheaper blowup dolls (pigs, lambs, etc.). Along the walls were row upon row of dirty dime novels and porn flicks to rent or buy. There was a small selection of lingerie—crotchless panties, peek-a-boo bras, novelty jockstraps. There were also ball gags, eye masks, and hundreds of vibrators, butt plugs, rubber fists, and dildos, including one that was three feet long and four inches thick (which was of course black). Sin City also had a large selection of fetish magazines, many imported and with price tags between sixty and one hundred dollars. They were the most valuable merchandise in the joint, and so right in front of the counter.

Many of Sin City's regulars seemed like relatively normal guys—downtown hipsters with kids, slick lawyers, gleaners who came in to unload fenced goods—but mostly the place was frequented by lonely unemployed men looking for company and/or a good cocksucking. Women who came in, with the exception of the occasional drunken bachelorette party, were always prostitutes.

Sin City functioned as a sort of coffee shop hangout for many of these folks. They brought in donuts and the newspaper and hung out with Pink for hours, working on the crossword puzzle. Occasionally they'd buy a few whip-its and get a handjob in the back.

Sex is so strangely innocent. The feces of polite society gets heaped on it constantly, yet it remains a relatively pure thing, a simple hunger that needs sating.

That many of the guys at Sin City had just plain given up was clear. Who wants to hunt for another ornery, expensive bitch with a crotch between her legs? Sin City offered a more up-front alternative. Get a handful of quarters, head to the arcade, stuff enough coins in the slot for a lunch break's worth of porn, and sit back and enjoy the hundred channels featuring all your favorites—mostly late seventies and early eighties shot-on-film stuff, lots of threeways and gangbangs, girl-girl, gay and animal porn, and some fancy fetish crap. Undo your pants and let your imagination run wild. There was always a hungry mouth on the other side of the wall should you care to have your cock massaged by something other than your own hand. More than likely the mouth belonged to a lonely old man, but who could say for sure? When you were finished, you could go up to the front desk where Pink was, listening to the new Cat Power CD and working on his bicycle, and pretend that you really came in to buy flavored condoms.

Pink was always the only guy on duty. Thus if someone OD'd or smeared shit all over a video stall or if a fight broke out, he had to deal with it. One time a guy rented a private room for an hour. When he hadn't come out after ninety minutes, Pink went to check on him. The man was wearing a wig and had stretched fishnets over his legs, arms, face, and torso and smeared mascara over his entire body. The poor guy was on the floor sobbing when Pink kicked in the door and threw him out.

Pink was full of stories like this when he got off work at eleven at night. Hearing him tell them in his inimitable world-weary way was the highlight of our nights, so Mona and I frequently made the effort to meet him at the shop. Then the three of us would bicycle over to Fellini and listen to his war stories over pints of Red Hook IPA.

Tonight, though, Mona and I also had to work.

After the suit from the coffee shop took us to the movie, we walked Pink to Sin City. Mona tried in vain to get our ringer to buy her the new *SKINTWO* magazine (our friend Raven was on the cover) but he didn't bite. Fine. We'd settle for drinks.

We walked up 3rd Avenue towards Columbia Street to the Veritable Quandary, a swanky bar known for its wonderful hot drinks. We all got mimosas followed by strong Spanish coffees. Then Mona remembered her to-do list.

"Shit! I've got to pick up the liquid latex at the Future today! Shit! Do you have a car?"

This last line she purred while running her fingers down the ringer's lapel. We gulped down our 151-and-coffee concoctions as he paid the bill.

We dragged him up Washington Street to the Future, stopping

only twice more to try on expensive footwear at Johnny Sole and to look for top hats at the magic store. Everyone everywhere knew Mona. They wore a mix of dread and delight when she sashayed through their doorways, a born princess in pauper's clothing.

"Mona! Mona!!!"

Nikki had the *de rigueur* baby-voiced squeal of a veteran stripper, honed over ten-plus years on Mary's Club's tiny stage. She worked at the Future—a clothing boutique specializing in fetish wear, rocker threads, skinhead duds, and stripper stuff—as much for the social cachet as for the deep employee discount.

"Oh Mona! I saw your article in *PDXS*. Meow. It was SO HOT! Hey, Viva! You girls wanna get stooooned? Oh, shit. I hope Mandy didn't hear that..."

Mandy was just coming down from her upstairs office. She owned the Future and was the biggest cunt I'd ever met. That she was donating a gallon jug of liquid latex to our cause at cost really proved once and for all that Mona could get milk out of a stone. Mandy, with her fat white face and gratingly orange-red hair, was a sales dominatrix. NO ONE was allowed to leave her store without dropping a couple hundred dollars. She spotted the ringer quick as a cat and pounced on us.

"Everything in the store is twenty percent off. That rack of stuff there is all clearance."

Mona's arms were already heaped with Catherine Coatney outfits to try on for our mark who was, it must be said, enjoying himself heartily. I picked through the clearance rack and found a five-dollar neon green ultra-miniskirt.

Suddenly the ringer caught wind of the time. He had to go, pronto. We made him buy the liquid latex and give us twenty bucks for a cab. We were beginning to sober up. Soon it would be seven o'clock and time to get drunk again.

Back at the Lawn I took a quick shower while Mona ran a bath. I was scared to death to be working a shift with her. I was generally still scared to death to go to work at all, but to work with Mona? Terrifying.

At half past seven she and I rode our bicycles to Fellini and ordered sidecars and hummus. The barmaid let us put our duffel bags behind the bar so we could make the necessary social butterfly rounds, kissing the cooks, the dishwashers, the wait staff, and Ivy.

Ivy was an older gentleman who bought and sold junked cars. He had a fondness for cocaine and was a fixture at Fellini and Satyricon, kinda like how your lecherous uncle is a fixture at Christmas dinner. He was having a beer with Elvis, a cross-eyed mentally challenged goliath who dressed up in a white rhinestone jumpsuit and performed all of Elvis's dance moves with a belligerent yell and a one-stringed guitar. It's probably good for a bar to have such dedicated patrons as Ivy and Elvis. That way it's one step closer to being a hang-out bar, cuz heck! Those two old guys are always there, hangin' out, rain or shine, whether you're new in town or have been around the block five hundred times. Ivy and Elvis were the seeds of our seedy community.

Soon it was 8:30. Mona and I paid our check, grabbed our bags, and rode our bikes two blocks to the Magic, wheeling them right inside the bar to the long hallway in back of the stage. I felt so tough, saddled with my huge stripper bag, biking everywhere, following this bald banshee all around town, hot on the trail of beauty, truth, and cheap lingerie.

It was Tuesday night and not very crowded. Jerry was bartending and made each of us a strong greyhound. I was nervous and sucked mine down fast. I knew Mo would make me go up first.

I preferred to start out the night in a bubbly, cheery mood, so I almost always debuted in a white skirt and fuzzy sweater. The white skirt/fuzzy sweater sexuality was light and flirtatious and much easier to conjure than the seductive siren shtick. Underneath I'd wear an ultra-innocent white cotton bra and panties and, on my feet, clunky holographic seven-inch clogs. I was very cute, which was the most I could hope for up against Mona's take-no-prisoners vamp.

I selected four cute and bubbly songs for my first set: Adam Ant's "Goody Two Shoes," the Cars' "My Best Friend's Girl," Butter 08's "Butter of 69," and for the finale, Bow Wow Wow's "I Want Candy." Delightful. That soundtrack combined with being onstage would get me smiling and giggling in no time. That soundtrack plus me smiling and giggling plus my short white skirt would endear me to ninety percent of the clientele (the other ten percent was just there to play video poker). So much I had already figured out.

I was often quite nervous for my first set. I'd dance too fast, spin around too much, jabber on maniacally, and gawk in shock when I caught my own eye in the stage mirrors. But four songs later I'd be in performance mode, feeling no pain, no shame. I figured the guys would appreciate it if they knew I got a bit of stage fright in their honor. Many strippers said they still got butterflies after as much as fifteen years. In "legitimate" theater, it's said that the day you don't get butterflies and the attendant adrenaline rush is the day you should hang it up. Did Mona get butterflies, I wondered?

When my short bubbly set was done, I abashedly picked up the one-dollar bills that littered the rack and stage, thanking each and every gentleman three and four times profusely for "supporting the arts." One fellow had a ten-dollar bill in front of him. He was a greasy biker who looked like he'd been drinking all day—definitely not the big spender type. I figured he'd made a mistake. Like an idiot, I told him so.

"Hey, hon. I think you meant to put down a one."

"No, that's for you baby. You earned it."

I blushed through my pancake makeup and clutched my robe to my chest. Bad stripper! Bad, bad stripper! Take the money and run! I wondered if I'd ever feel comfortable accepting money from people.

On my way back to the dressing room, I caught a glimpse of a cute guy sitting alone on a corner barstool as far as he could get from the stage. He met my glance but then quickly stared into his beer. I sauntered over and asked him his name. He mumbled something that sounded like "Fred."

I've got a weakness for shy boys. Weakness isn't perhaps the right word, because I devour them. Poor Fred. The rest of the evening I toyed with him mercilessly.

He was painfully awkward; he even stuttered when he spoke. I got the feeling he'd rather be dead than deal with my advances, but I rather enjoyed torturing him. After every set I made a point of saying something mildly salacious to him.

Slowly—as slowly as a thawing lake—Fred's reluctance began to crack. Eventually he inched his way the long ten feet to my rack, where he sat doodling desperately on napkins to avoid my stare. Of course he was an artist. His napkins looked like they might have been pinched from the Picasso Museum in Barcelona—lots of an-gular abstract faces surrounded by weird podlike flowers that were vaguely vaginal.

"So, Fred, what's your sign?" I asked, reclining in front of him on the brass rail wearing only my white lace thong.

"Libra," he mumbled, barely audible, but I heard it.

I all but fell off the rail. "Looks like you're coming home with me tonight."

Lovesick fool. Here I was three years later, still swooning over boys who reminded me of my high school sweetheart, also a shy, enig-matic Libra. I'd already bedded one patron this way—a guy with dark hair and dark eyes like my old paramour. He probably had a name, too. When I asked him his sign and he responded Libra, I shook my head resignedly and said, "Looks like you won the lottery." That was the first and second-to-last boy I'd bed from the bar. Fred would be the last.

By the time Fred had finally made it to my stage, it was 2 AM. Closing time. Only a couple other guys remained as I retreated to the dressing room to put on my street clothes. When I reappeared, Fred was still hanging around.

"Did you drive here?" I asked him.

"No, I missed the last bus..." Of course he didn't have a car.

"We'll walk to my house. It's only fourteen blocks away."

I tried to make small talk with the poor boy but he had evi-dently been stricken mute. Thank God Mona was walking her bike home, too.

Back at the Lawn I said goodnight to Mo and carried my bike and my bag up the stairs to my new shithole apartment, #216. Fred, like a stray dog, followed cautiously about four paces behind.

Inside my apartment I lit a few candles and turned on the Christ-mas lights that decorated the stairs to my "playroom"—a sleeping loft covered with three mattresses and heaps of blankets and pillows, ringed with mirrors and a poster of Led Zeppelin's *Houses of the Holy*. I slipped out of my clothes one last time and into my kimono. I grabbed a stack of pictures and climbed the ladder to the playroom where I lit more candles. Fred stood awkwardly in the darkened room, his hands stuffed in his pockets.

"Come here, Mr. Libra. Don't be so darn shy. I wanna show you some pictures."

He took off his shoes and his shirt and climbed up to the loft. He was so skinny he looked in danger of disappearing.

"Isn't it cozy up here? It's my playroom."

I flipped through the photos by candlelight—old pictures of my family, of college chums, of travels in Africa and Asia. I figured that if I gave Fred a glimpse of my real life he might open up just a crack. Who knew where it could lead? I was awfully attracted to his long skinny body and big scared blue-gray eyes, his mop of soft brown hair forever falling in them.

He looked at the photos intently but still made no moves. Jesus Christ. So I did, kissing him tenderly. Instantly he turned ravenous. I *knew* it! Shy boys are all so pent-up.

We groped and bit and licked and chewed on each other, making a disaster area of the playroom. But when I grabbed a condom out of my little antique glass jewelry case, there was precious little to wrap it around. Fred was evidently wasted. Whiskey dick. My first encounter. I tried to make light of the situation as he tried desperately to squish his little semi into me. Ugh. I wanted it to be over. I wanted to be sitting with Pink at the drag queen breakfast counter on Vaseline Alley, laughing at my misadventures over enormous blueberry pancakes and mugs of truck-stop coffee. How much longer 'til sunrise? Eventually we both passed out.

I woke up a short while later because the playroom was on fire. Some deep survival-minded part of my brain conquered the alcohol and exhaustion and resuscitated me just in time. I stared for a couple seconds, thinking how beautiful it was to be in a bed on fire. Then I woke up Fred.

They say the Lawn would burn to the ground in three minutes if any of the structure caught fire. It was a total tinderbox. One time one of the many whores who turned tricks in the basement lit a mattress on fire while smoking crack. Three fire trucks showed up and we tenants were kept outside in our pajamas and, at four in the morning, lectured on how the place would burn down in three minutes, as if it was our fault there were whores turning tricks and smoking crack in the basement.

But now here I was, burning down the house. The heat of Fred's and my unconsummated passion was threatening the whole building.

The fire was lovely, warm, comforting, and cinematic. Fred doused it with a bottle of water and then smothered it with a blanket. Many of the photographs of my old life were singed and stuck together, but otherwise there was little damage. We went back to sleep. In the morning I pretended I had a doctor's appointment to get him out the door.

Fred kind of shadowed me from then on, but never really spoke. I tired of him quickly, and a week after our initial fiery encounter, I walked him to the river's edge and dumped him.

For years afterward I'd see him occasionally, wandering around in traffic, stumbling into moving vehicles. His friends said I really messed him up. For a long while I figured him for dead. But then he'd reappear at the Magic, desperately doodling cubist vaginas on cocktail napkins and trying to win me back.

Jesus Christ, Part One

One of the great perks of stripping is the delicious sleep that comes after an exhausting five-hour shift.

Only two girls worked the stage per shift at the Magic. That meant that over five hours, each performed approximately ten fifteen-minute sets of four songs, a total of forty emotionally, physically, and mentally challenging performances. I'd been an actress all my life and had performed on some pretty grand stages, but not even my leading roles compared with the intense focus and connection that stripping required. At the end of each shift I was so drained that the thought of one last costume change—into my street clothes—was often unbearable.

Somehow I'd summon the strength to pull on my blue jeans, my socks, and my boots, walk my bike out of the Magic, and ride the fifteen blocks up Couch Street past the brewery and the cathedral to the Lawn. Then, in a somnambulistic trance, I'd scrub off all the makeup and glitter, climb the ladder to my loft, and slide between the sheets. Every muscle ached, every bone felt bruised, but my soul was satisfied and my heart swollen with contentment. I'd fall asleep before my head hit the pillow and sleep the sleep of the dead.

But not the night of Monique's circus stunt.

I'd been asleep maybe two hours when I awoke with a start. A siren had perforated my dreams. I sat up in bed straining my ears. Outside the first rain of fall fell softly, but flashing red lights filled my room.

I climbed down from my loft and wrapped my kimono around me. Just as I went to open the door, someone knocked. Pink.

"Viva!" he whispered loudly. "The Jehovah's Witness jumped off the roof!"

Most of the Lawn's tenants were already milling around on the porch in their bathrobes. An ambulance and a fire truck lit up the night. Pink and I rushed to the front stairs just in time to see Monique being wheeled away on a stretcher, fighting against the restraints like a devil. She was covered in blood. Mona, wrapped in a red terry cloth robe, cried like she'd lost her own sister.

"What the hell happened?"

"Jackson said she took a whole bag of mushrooms and freaked out. She jumped out his window. Most of her teeth were knocked out." Marc, the sweetheart who lived on the third floor, had taken it upon himself to hold onto Monique until the paramedics came. He had blood all over his hands and shirt.

I wondered what drove Monique to down a whole bag of 'shrooms. A twenty-year-old waif of a girl, she was very religious, tightly wound, and supremely straight-edge. She'd never had a drink or a cigarette in her life. I looked around for Jackson—the drug-dealing, ticket-scalping hippie from the third floor. He was the only person likely to know what the fuck was going on, but like every other time there was a drug casualty at the Lawn, Jackson was mysteriously absent.

The ambulance drove off into the night and the slumber party moved back into the lobby. Mona and I followed Pink to his room, where we sat in silence until I decided to try and go back to bed. I set my alarm for 9 AM. For the first time in almost a year, I would be going to church. My life was getting a little too freaky.

When the alarm went off I lay in bed for a few minutes, replaying in my head the events of the night before. Marc had said that Monique was likely paralyzed. I felt partly responsible. Maybe stripping was indeed an unforgivable sin. Maybe the gods had thrown Monique out the window as a warning to me to clean up my shit.

As I crawled out of bed I felt a peculiar twinge of stage fright. Evidently going to church was going to be a performance.

The morning sun seemed unseasonably hot for fall. I rifled through my limited wardrobe and settled on a vintage baby-blue baby doll slip I'd bought at a thrift store. It was short and diaphanous and not at all church-going material. I felt rather like the whore of Babylon, though, and wanted to dress the part. I ferreted around in the shoe pile for my matching vintage Chanel knockoff sandals, then smiled delightedly at my reflection in the mirror. I looked adorable, feminine and sexy. The new me was armed and ready to contend with my history.

I munched on an apple on the way to Immanuel Lutheran and couldn't avoid its symbolism. Eve had been cast out of the Garden of Eden for eating the fruit of the Tree of Knowledge. Stripping seemed something of a parallel. I felt enlightened in my new career, like the wool had been pulled from over my eyes. I doubted that God would be pissed at me for dancing around naked, but I wasn't sure. My father, however, would be furious.

A block from the church my stomach turned into a flock of butterflies. At the entrance I kept walking, deciding to scrap the whole idea. I'd go across the street and pray for my salvation in private at Junkie Park. But my knockoff Chanel sandals did a one-eighty against my will and I soon found myself walking up Immanuel's red-carpeted stairs towards a welcoming usher.

Goddamnit, why had I insisted on wearing what amounted to a negligee? I felt terribly self-conscious. The usher didn't seem to mind, just handed me a bulletin. I passed the sanctuary and headed for the all-but-empty balcony, feeling that enlightened sex workers probably ought to be segregated from polite folk.

The inside of the church was, strangely, baby blue. My outfit matched perfectly! The bloodred carpets looked especially bloody in contrast to the pastel walls. My inner anthropologist mixed with my inner child as I started to deconstruct the familiar and comforting rituals of my childhood. But when the organ struck the first notes of the opening hymn, a sob welled up out of nowhere.

My dad and I had had it out long ago. The eldest and most headstrong of his four children, I was also the only daughter. He and I fought constantly. The problem was that he knew everything and I knew everything.

When I was eight years old I once insisted on wearing jeans to church. They were cute jeans—more knickers—which I paired with a stylish blue-and-white striped blouse that had puffed sleeves and a little necktie. I thought I looked great. My dad, who was then pastor at a large parish in Wisconsin, said I couldn't wear jeans to church. I refused to change my clothes and so the family left without me. Feeling I'd betrayed him utterly, I rode my bike the mile to church, holding back the tears. Then I sat in the balcony alone, in my blue jeans, and silently begged my father for forgiveness. Eight years old and cast out already!

Now, fourteen years later, I was that eight-year-old all over again, bleary-eyed and begging my dad for forgiveness from a church balcony.

The sobs welled up throughout the service. I knew all the prayers and liturgies by heart. When it was time for communion, I steeled myself for the walk down the red carpet in my ridiculous dress. Perhaps the communion wine would burn my throat like acid. Maybe lightning would strike me dead. But as the Holy Spirit accepted Mary Magdalene at its altar, so it accepted me.

"The Body of Christ, given for you."

My mouth was so dry I nearly choked on the wafer.

"Blood of Christ, shed for you."

I could've used a bit more wine. I lingered at the altar for a while, praying for guidance and for Monique, and thanking all of heaven for being so understanding about everything.

Finally the postlude played, an airy Bach cantata I'd learned on the piano as a child and taught myself on guitar in college. I walked home contemplative. This whore of Babylon thing really didn't suit me at all. Stripping was a walk on the wild side, sure, but my feeling I'd traded my clothes for a scarlet letter was just more unnecessary socialization bullshit. Even as a stripper I was still my daddy's little girl. I knew it, God knew it, and I had faith that one day even Dad would understand.

Life Oughtta Be a Cabaret II

Monique returned to the Lawn after two weeks in the hospital with a neck brace and most of her teeth glued back in her mouth. Already the existential crisis inspired by her high dive was ancient history. What surprised me most on seeing her again was how normal strangeness had become. My new life as an exotic dancer seemed less exotic every day.

Increasingly it seemed that the rest of Portland shared my sentiment. The buzz generated by Mona's cabaret was fast becoming the talk of the town, and even the politically correct newsweeklies were hungry for copy from us. So one drizzly October afternoon, Teresa, Rain, Pink, Mo, and I met in Chinatown to take some publicity photos to promote her first cabaret at the Magic Gardens.

Mo recruited one of her lackeys to shoot us; the idea was a Frank Miller tribute. Comic artist Frank Miller drew a fab series called *Sin City*. Its heroes were strippers and prostitutes. Each woman was skilled in martial arts or poisons or knife throwing or whatnot, so for the photo shoot Mona wore a fake fur dress and matching feather wig and wielded a machete and a cigarette. Teresa wore a G-string and a fringed bra, a little knife duct-taped to her arm, and a length of chain over her shoulder. Rain Stormm—who worked at the Magic and was by now an integral member of our gang—sported chaps, a vest, and a neck kerchief and carried toy pistols. I wore a bunny outfit from Frederick's of Hollywood and rocked a lead pipe and a smirk. Pink wore a suit and carried an umbrella.

The grainy black-and-white images of the five of us posing menacingly on drug-addled 4th Avenue were not the usual stripper pinups or club advertisements. The press ate it up and the cabaret got previews in

JUNE 29TH

COME SEE
Miss Mona's
LADIES OF
LEISURE
CABARET
FEATURING
RAIN
STORM

BERBATI'S PAN • 231 SW ANKENY

all the local rags, which was impressive for a show at a dive strip bar in Chinatown, still very much a no man's land. Slowly a new crowd of artists, musicians, punk rockers, and hipsters trickled into the Magic to see what the buzz was about.

You never knew what you might see at Miss Mona's cabarets. Each involved considerable planning and research, culminating in a frothy mix of classic vintage acts like the balloon dance or the feather dance, mixed with utterly bizarre scenes that tread the outer boundaries of taste. Whether in conversation, during cabarets, or merely working the afternoon shift, Mona always challenged her audience, which in the late-twentieth century was no easy feat. Her ultimate stage fantasy was to have a girl dressed as a cat pee in a litter box. I've no doubt she would've shot herself onstage if it hadn't already been done in the '70s by Chris Burden.

Mona's cabarets went far beyond the usual talent show burlesque. She was a visionary and a dictator. She could, through sheer force of personality, get all the strippers to the bar by noon on Sunday and get the boss to hand over the keys. Flunkies made elaborate costumes and props. Several girls were recruited to be gal Fridays on stage-managing detail. It's not easy to herd divas around a cramped basement, kitchen, and dressing room, making sure they're on stage on time with the requisite boa constrictor, whipped cream, or mattress. Gal Fridays also helped girls wash off body paint, liquid latex, glitter, and foodstuffs in the large industrial kitchen sinks. Their most fearsome task, however, was enabling Mona—taking her shit, wiping her shit, loving her shit.

For every cabaret staged, a mutiny was threatened. Mona was a cunt—yelling, screaming, pulling out her nonexistent hair, chain-smoking, chewing her nonexistent nails. She managed to get us all to work for free to flesh out her weird fantasies and then abused us mightily. Every time we'd swear "Never again," but when the next organizational meeting rolled around, we'd sign on in spite of ourselves. Collectively we were out of this world.

For the first cabarets, before I'd proven my mettle, Mona cast me as Bunny Girl. Mostly this meant I worked the CD player, but eventually I was allowed to take the stage to play Twister with audience members and finally to debut my first self-authored performance, which involved the bunny outfit, lots of Hostess products, and a strobe light.

As Mona's confidence in me grew, so did my stage time. Soon I'd morphed from Bunny Girl to Songbird, singing a sultry jazz version of Kiss's "I Wanna Rock 'n' Roll All Night" before ransacking the stripper songbook for X-rated versions of Marilyn Monroe and Marlene Dietrich standards.

Mona's performances were, as usual, psychosexual warfare. For her first Magic cabaret, she did a quick change from heartless dressing-room Hitler to serene geisha. Her boys had built her an actual sedan chair on the front porch of the Lawn. In borrowed suits, they carried her in state to the stage. Bowie's "China Girl" played, of course. She peered shyly through the red and gold curtains of her coach as they set it down onstage, then slowly, daintily emerged. Her face was a mask of pancake make-up and perfectly drawn geisha features and she wore my new hundred-fifty-dollar vintage 1920s kimono, tied with a ruby-hued sash.

Mona did her signature Mona, barely moving at all, but seductively and with impossible grace. Slowly she unwrapped the red sash and let the kimono fall to the floor. Then, with subtle Oriental agony, she stabbed herself with a long machete, wrapped in red ribbons, through the heart. She collapsed on the stage covered in fake blood and real tears, her post-partum freakout commencing before the curtain even fell. She had to be carried home where, three days later, she emerged with sketches for her next acid dream made flesh, Miss Mona's XXXmas.

Truth be told, there wasn't much Christmassy about Miss Mona's XXXmas, but we did recruit Rain to be Santa's little helper. She was perfect for the part.

Impossibly effervescent, smiley and sweet, Rain Stormm was a born stripper. She slayed more hearts than the rest of us combined, dancing nimbly to the Beastie Boys with her long brown hair, big brown eyes, and classically beautiful wide round face.

Rain was born and raised in the Pacific Northwest and was quintessentially of the place. She had dropped out of high school; she was wonderfully smart but just couldn't hack being cooped up like that. She took modeling classes and dance lessons. She began stripping at twenty and was instantly a hit. Her giggles and air kisses effortlessly kept the storm clouds away from herself and her patrons. She was the girl next door, America's sweetheart, and was Magic's reigning queen for many years. She was also a terrible drunk.

The night of the cabaret, Rain was dressed to kill, wearing an elf outfit and antlers. I was wedged in the corner DJ area, sweating bullets at the thought of taking the stage to play Twister. The Magic was a teeny tiny bar in an urban wasteland. I'd been on much bigger stages all over the country as an actress, dancer, and musician, but the little Magic stage felt so exalted to me on cabaret nights that I was completely petrified. I took a customer up on a shot of Jägermeister to steel myself for the short walk to the stage, my heart thump-thump-thumping as I maneuvered through the packed bar in my bunny outfit that amounted to three strategically-placed cotton balls.

"Who wants to play Twister with Viva Las Vegas, the naughtiest little wabbit? Think your Twister twists are any match for her curvy curves?" the barker barked, as I suggestively rubbed up against him. Once onstage I blossomed into a million points of light. Why? I was just playing Twister semi-nude with audience members. What was the big deal? But the gaze of the crowd was so intoxicating that I felt like I was levitating. It's good to levitate when you're playing Twister. You're sure to win!

Meanwhile, Rain was helping a lot of Santas. She was perched precariously on a guy's lap in the corner, throwing back the last of her Razzatini. She giggled wildly as she made her way to the bar for another one, but stumbled on the stair by the CD player and cancelled the music cued up for the next act. "Whoops!" More giggling. "Where did I leave my drink? Did I leave it downstairs? Does anyone have any P-O-T?"

Rain, inebriated, managed to navigate the steep, broken stairway in seven-inch stilettos and passed out on the dressing room floor midway through our first show. After my glorious first foray onstage I came downstairs to total chaos. Somehow Rain's passing out was my fault. Mona was screaming at me. What were we going to do without Santa's little helper for the second show?

Rain slept peacefully through the melee, a little smile on her perfect Cupid's bow lips.

"Mona, she's at least out of the way now. Santa can help himself."

Mo was irate. But it was time to get her ready for her mermaid act, so we slid her, screaming, into her long, scaly, custom-made tail. Her body was covered with black liquid latex, making the whites of her eyes and gnashing teeth look especially menacing as she cursed and carried on. The boys in the hallway came in to calm her down. A joint was passed while I hustled back to my DJ corner to make sure Mona's PJ Harvey CD—the one she stole from me—was ready to go.

Mona channeled her wrath into her performance, writhing around for a long, pulsating, guitar-driven song. At the end, in what was becoming a theme, she took a huge knife and plunged it into her lower abdomen. She sliced through her thick scaly tail and slowly wiggled her long legs free. Her eyes glowed in the red lights of the stage, the rest of her an inky, scary black. She ran her little pink tongue along her upper lip while staring down a poor soul at the rack. The song ended. I put in the *Best of Bowie*, hit random, and beat it to the basement to do damage control.

Rain! She was taking up half the small downstairs dressing room, stretched out rigidly, naked, like a corpse. What was I supposed to do with her? Say "Get the fuck up, get pretty, and get onstage"? She was passed out! Mona needed a miracle worker on staff. If I could just weather the tirade without snapping back, by the next morning everything would be fine. Mo wouldn't remember a thing and Rain would be giggling through a double Bloody Mary breakfast. But that was a lifetime away and my nerves were already raw.

Thank God June was down there, washing creamed corn off of Morgan Le Fay who had just wrestled Lawyer Patty in a kiddie pool filled with the crap. With June's help, I stuffed Rain into a corner of the dressing room for the second half of the show. Finally, at the end of the night, while onstage a demented Santa spanked a phalanx of bare-butted vixens, we smuggled Rain out and loaded her into her pickup. Pink—in his Mr. Pink tuxedo and hat—drove us all to the Lawn. We carried her up the stairs and laid her on my couch with a blanket. She came to for a minute, giggling.

"Veeeva! Veeeevahh, I luuuuv you."

Jesus, Rain. If I had an award to give out to the greatest stripper I've ever met, I'd give it to you, honey.

Bunny

It was the best of times. Life wasn't exactly easy street, but every day was a movable feast and the future looked fabulous. Still I knew that it wouldn't last, couldn't last, that it was just a matter of time before the bubble burst. Things were a little too good.

I decided to go home for Christmas. It broke my heart to leave Portland, but if I had one directive in my soul, it was to keep on truckin'. Plus I wanted to see my family.

I booked a train to Minnesota. I would go for three weeks. That'd give me a chance to relax, have a nice butt-tightening ski vacation, and explore a new strip club: fabulous old Club Saratoga in scenic downtown Duluth.

As the train pulled out of Portland's Union Station, I surveyed the desolate wasteland of railyards and bridges twinkling in the gunmetal twilight. It looked like the dreariest Christmas ever, but I was blinded by love. I loved Portland, loved Mona, loved stripping, loved life. I felt so grateful to have found my little niche that I folded my hands to thank God in an epic prayer. When Prince's "Purple Rain" came on over my headphones I cried, overcome with emotion.

"Dear Lord, thank you for bringing me to this distant no man's land. Thank you for leading me to Mona and Pink, Teresa and the Magic. Thank you for putting me down in a place where my voice and my opinions resonate. Let me have a safe journey home, a fulfilling time with my family, and let me come back refreshed for the work you have for me here. Also, please take good care of my cat."

Two days later the train pulled into St. Paul, where I transferred to a bus. By late afternoon I was waiting for my dad to pick me up at the Greyhound station in Duluth.

He was late, as usual, and so left his Subaru running as he bounded towards me and enveloped me in a huge bear hug. My heart tightened ominously in my chest as I felt the familiar scratch of his Norwegian wool sweater against my face. I knew then that I had committed some kind of betrayal, that no matter how righteous I felt about my new career, it was never going to be okay with my dad. The Reverend might one day understand my choices, but the daddy never would.

THE MAGIC GARDEN

OPEN DAILY 12 NOON TO 2 AM OPEN SUNDAY AT 6PM

Miss Mona's

XXX-mas Special Cabaret

DECEMBER 8TH

Where Badness is really Good!

DOORS OPEN AT 6PM ★ FIRST SHOW AT 9PM
LATE SHOW AT 11:30PM

DAILY LUNCH SPECIAL KITCHEN OPEN 'TIL 2AM

217 NW 4TH IN HISTORIC CHINATOWN (503) 224-8472

He took me to a malt shop across the street from the bus station and asked me a little bit about my job as a cocktail waitress over fish & chips and barley soup. Clearly Mom hadn't told him about my actual nine-to-five. I simply wasn't ready for Dad's reaction. He and I had argued like trial lawyers throughout my childhood, and knew well where to hit each other so that it really hurt. Loathe to lie about my new career, I told him tersely that cocktail waitressing paid the bills, then changed the subject. I asked about the weather, which provided conversation for the rest of the meal and the drive home.

A blanket of snow three feet deep covered the town. It crunched under the wheels of the car as we turned off the interstate onto Highway 61, Lake Superior looming large on the right, dark and mysterious on the frigid, moonlit night.

Back at the house Mom had gone all-out with the Christmas décor. She was obviously happy to have her whole brood together: even her two little terriers sported festive Christmas bows. They attacked me the moment I walked in the door. I lay down on the carpet and let them cover my face with kisses, exhausted after my long journey.

"Hooray, you're here! Boys!! Your sister's home!"

I reluctantly threw the dogs off me and hugged my mom and my three rogue brothers. Although I was the eldest, the boys all towered over me; even the baby—now fourteen—had inched past me in the last year.

Dad mixed gin and tonics as my brothers carried my bags to my room. As soon as they'd all retreated to the basement to watch TV, I called for my mom. I had carried a duffel bag of stripper duds all the way from Portland and was ecstatic to show them to her. It never occurred to me that she might be horrified.

"Mom, you've gotta check this stuff out! Look at these shoes!" I pulled out my favorite seven-inch wood and leopard platforms. "Aren't these awesome? And really they're so comfortable."

"Oh, hon! Honestly." She covered her eyes with her hands as if that might make it all go away.

I dumped the whole bag out on my childhood four-poster princess bed: the G-strings, the BABE panties, the disco ball dress, and the royal blue kimono from Goodwill. My new Lycra wardrobe mixed with my Norwegian sweaters and polypropylene skiwear.

"Look at this! And this!"

"Oh, gosh. I can't believe you're doing this. I don't want to see this."

Mom was always able to put some teeth into "Oh gosh." It stung. She was not impressed.

"But Mom, I love this stuff. I love dancing. I brought all this home to show you!"

She had always tried to dress me up like a girl in dresses and lacy things. I was a tomboy and rebelled mightily. Now I had dresses and heels! She ought to have been thrilled.

"Oh, honestly. I've got to finish the dishes."

She was pissed alright. I put everything away, totally deflated. She'd seemed okay with the idea of stripping six months ago, when we'd taken long walks on Lake Superior and I'd told her all the ideological musings on body and culture, feminism, and prostitution I'd conjured at college senior year. Now, though, she was dead set against it.

The next night I snuck out into the bitter cold and dragged my duffel bag downtown to audition at Club Saratoga, the strip club I'd visited the summer before. I'd purposely booked an extended stay in Duluth, hoping to pick up a few shifts at the 'Toga and make enough money to pay my January rent.

I was excited about working at a new club. The Saratoga had a glorious speakeasy vibe, as if it were a relic from the 1920s when Northern Minnesota was a vacation paradise frequented by the likes of Babe Ruth. Its bar was a magnificent five-tiered affair—bottles of booze were stacked to the ceiling, twinkling in the light of red-velvet-covered hanging lamps. Along the back wall were photos of strippers from the fifties, sixties, and seventies. There was also a giant nautical chart of Lake Superior. A little old lady with white hair and gold-rimmed glasses collected the two-dollar cover charge and checked IDs at the front door, her head otherwise buried in a giant library book. Another little old lady worked the gambling desk inside. In the very back, by the pool tables, was a darling bar diorama which featured a dozen taxidermic squirrels playing cards, drinking pints, and brawling.

Club Saratoga had a full bar and all-nude chicks, something increasingly rare in America, where modern-day morality drew the line at enjoying a soda with your skin. The club was one of only two in

Minnesota that allowed booze and nudity; it had been around so long that it was grandfathered in when new decency laws were passed. The dancers at the 'Toga were primarily circuit girls—strippers who travel around the country doing week-long or longer residencies at far-flung strip joints. There were also some local single moms who said they were thirty-seven but looked much older. One of these, upon hearing I was from Portland, said she'd never work there, that every stripper in Portland was a drug-addicted prostitute.

Another girl, tall and gorgeous with pale white skin, long black ringlets, and knee-high black boots, told me she had two PhDs and three masters degrees, owned houses in New York, Montana, and somewhere else, and had paid for it all—time and money—by stripping. That's what she said, at least. I of course believed her.

My naïveté worked well for me in dressing rooms. Even prima donnas thawed a bit when presented with my self-deprecating sense of humor and a compliment on their lipstick. Frequently they'd open up a tad and even take me into confidence, dishing dirt on the other dames. The older, more hard-bitten strippers were easy, too: after a cursory glance at the photos of the smiling kids that decorated her stripper bag, I'd rave about how cute her kid/grandkid was or how I loved the bedazzled red unitard she'd worn for her last set. These older ladies would never open up, but they'd at least clear a little corner for me on the vanity. I considered such tiny victories all-out triumphs.

I performed a festive Santa Baby number for my audition, starting things off in my black catsuit, then stripping down to red sheer panties, tiny tits, and Santa hat to a soundtrack of Christmas hits. The Duluthians—a rather rough crowd—seemed perplexed. They were accustomed to more overtly sexual dancers and probably hadn't seen coy since 1962. Still they came to the rack with dollars in their mouths. Protocol at the 'Toga dictated that every gal take the guy's dollar from his mouth with her tits, allowing him a good sniff and nuzzle along the way. No way, José. Instead I'd lean shyly into a guy and whisper in his ear, full of suggestion, "Why don't you be a gentleman and just put that down at my rack?" Or, breathy as could be, "You know you can get hepatitis that way."

After my set I threw my gear back into my bag as a Mötley Crüe song roared through the club and one of the thirty-seven-year-olds took the stage. I gave five bucks to each of the strippers and tipped the bar ten, pocketing thirty-four. The nice lady bartender poured me a whiskey with hot water on the house as I accepted a congratulatory cigarette from the gentleman sitting next to me. No longer jittery with stage fright, I noticed that there was a lesbian couple enjoying the show amidst the blue-collar boys and bachelor party. There was also a large handwritten sign advertising "Live Jazz Every Saturday." I had to hand it to Duluth; it was more sophisticated than I'd thought.

I gave my name and phone number to the bartender and told her I'd be in town through January 2nd and would like to work as much as possible. Then I wrapped my thick wool scarf around my neck, zipped my little white Eskimo jacket up to my chin, hoisted my stripper bag over my shoulder, and headed for home, tired but elated with the post-stripping glow. Unfortunately World War III greeted me around the Christmas tree.

Somehow Daddy had caught wind of where I'd been and what I was doing. When Mom saw the lights of the Subaru turn into the driveway, she rushed outside to head me off at the pass.

"Your brothers told your father where you were and boy is he pissed. I'm pissed, too. You can do what you want in Portland but keep it out of our house!"

I glared at her defensively, like a preteen who'd been told to take off her mascara and lipstick. Clearly this crisis was my parents' own damn fault; if they could just be a little more open-minded!

Suddenly my father's voice pierced the silent night. He was screaming.

"You're a WHORE! I want you out of this house and don't come back! You're arousing temptation! You're encouraging lust! Don't let me see your face again until you've admitted the error of your ways!"

Jesus Christ. I'd never heard him curse using such Old Testament language before; usually it was all New Testament forgiveness stuff around our house. I was stunned. I could tell how heartbroken he was. I never wanted to hurt him. All of a sudden I was heartbroken, too. I crawled back into the car, freezing cold in the sub-zero night, turned on the radio while running down the battery and wailed like a banshee.

"There's no place like home…there's no place like home," I howled, with Bonnie Raitt's "Have a Heart" playing loud on the stereo.

Where was home? It sure as hell wasn't Duluth, and it sure as hell wasn't my father's house. I wanted to take the next train back to Portland, Pink, and Mona.

A short while later my mom came out to drag me back into the house. My eyes were all but swollen shut. She looked like she'd been crying, too. I quietly got ready for bed, sponging off the smeared mascara and Revlon ColorStay lipstick. My dad was still yelling in the basement. I felt horrible, my insides turned to stone. I wished with all my heart I was back in Portland. Yeah, these people were blood; yeah, they had raised me. But they'd never understand me.

No one breathed a word about my new career after that, and I gave up on the idea of trying new stages while I was in Duluth. This meant I was flat broke and would be hard-pressed for rent, so I took over my baby brother's paper route to earn a little cash.

Every morning, long before the sun rose, I walked a couple miles around the neighborhood in snow up to my chest. On warmer mornings the temperature got up to -20°. Cold days were -40° (-80° with the windchill). This crumpled my cocksure lickety-split. I got very sad and lonely.

Then, a few days after Christmas, Pink called.

"Mona got fired from the Magic. She's lost her mind completely. She freaked out and threw an ashtray at a customer and hit him in the head. Grandpa eighty-sixed her. Now she's getting evicted."

The end was already at hand. I tried frantically to call Mona but I couldn't reach her; her phone had been cut off. I felt somehow to blame. I shouldn't have left.

After three weeks of icy, isolated hell in Northern Minnesota, I gingerly said goodbyes to my real family, my entire body aching to be back in the comforting embrace of my new family. Mom teared up at the Greyhound station, perhaps reading my mind: I wouldn't be returning to her house anytime soon.

The two-day train trip back to Portland was nothing like the serene self-satisfied voyage of three weeks prior. Whereas then I had been blissing out, ecstatic to have found my destiny and my tribe, my time in Duluth had sobered me up right good. The party was over. Mona had done a total Humpty Dumpty this time, and my smirk seemed to have migrated to my forehead, now furrowed constantly at the dreadful unfairness of it all…. That a people, a nation, the world so resisted being *saved*.

I finally caught up with Mona two days after I got back. She'd been staying with Rain when she wasn't at the bars.

"Oh, Viva! The most horrible thing happened. We were walking up East Burnside after drinking at the Galaxy when we saw this little white bunny loose on the street. We chased it and tried to stop traffic and finally we caught it, but it wriggled away and ran across the road and was killed right in front of us! Oh, Viva! It was an omen! A terrible, terrible omen. We must leave this town. This town is evil! Oh, Viva! Why did you go away?"

I suspected that the spell had broken; the good times were gone. I wasn't far from wrong. Soon everything would turn to shit in a horrible reverse alchemy.

The reign of Terri had begun.

Motherfucking Management Fucks It All Up

Terri was a little old lady who bartended nights at the Magic; she was the ugliest human being I had ever known, inside and out. She had frizzy red hair—curly on top and a stringy mullet on the sides—and looked as old as Moses, deep fissures in her orange-gray skin. She had black-brown eyes that revealed nothing. She lied, cheated, and stole. She chain-smoked menthols. Many customers liked her, taken in by her fake grin and strong pour. She was "nice" to some, hideous to others, and not consistent in either case. But she was consistently evil to strippers. She hated us more than anything—viewed us as one more stinking injustice in the stream of diarrhea that was her life. And man did we hate her.

Rumors swirled as to her backstory. What was clear was that she felt deeply indebted to Magic's owner, a man we called Grandpa. Grandpa was a suave sixty-something Harley Davidson aficionado who owned several bars. He was a kind and generous man, witty, naughty, and wise. You could sense this upon entering any of his establishments. The Magic, for instance, was primarily a comfortable and convivial hangout, *Cheers*-like, and only secondarily a strip club; a place where girls could be themselves and guys could enjoy the pleasure of their company for the price of a drink—a dollar seventy-five minimum.

According to legend, Grandpa and Terri started out as archrivals; Terri had her own restaurant two blocks away from a bar that Grandpa owned. One night there was a fire and she lost everything. Grandpa—in a typical display of generosity—bailed her out, hired her on as a waitress, and set her up in one of his rental houses. When Grandpa bought the Magic, he brought on Terri as night bartender. He trusted her and she felt obliged. She didn't like strip bars or strippers, but she was fatally loyal to Grandpa and would do whatever he asked.

At the time of my arrival at the Magic, Grandpa's wife had just succumbed to lung cancer after a long battle. For a couple of care-free months the scheduling of dancers and day-to-day management had been something of a free-for-all. But when Terri was installed as manager, things changed overnight. Several girls were canned immediately for no apparent reason, leaving the rest of us tiptoeing around in our stilettos, terrified that we too would lose our jobs. We learned quickly that to survive we must never question the tyrant's authority and—of course—pay a healthy tithe.

Soon it was common knowledge that to work at the Magic you not only had to endure Terri, you also had to kiss her ass. Always. This alone kept many girls from auditioning, even though the Magic became known as a great money club amongst dancers. We gals who did work there developed deep bonds, forged by our collective loathing of her. Still we necessarily became adept at kissing her wrinkled white ass.

I hate kissing ass. I hate all forms of lying, especially when it's piddly and forced. Martin Luther said, "If you are going to sin, sin boldly." If you must tell a lie, make it a good one. Not "Oh Terri, your hair looks so cute today! What is that delightful perfume you're wearing? Did you borrow that precious glitter nail polish from one of your brilliant granddaughters? How fabulous! Here—I baked some cookies today and thought you might like some."

Girls who got the best shifts were those who relied on Terri the most. And who tipped out the most. Girls brought her candy, perfume, flowers. They confided in her, moved in with her. She liked to have complete control, so junkies and felons became her favorites. Try to keep your head on your shoulders, stay relatively clean and sober and reliable, and you were bound to lose in the end. Eventually she would only give the cherry shifts to the addict girls, girls who would walk with two hundred dollars on a six-hundred-dollar Friday night shift. Terri kept the rest.

Terri did have a peculiar aesthetic that went over well with the hipster contingent, and one that ultimately set the Magic apart from the more stereotypical strip clubs: Terri did not like breast augmentation. In Portland's saturated strip club scene, boob jobs were the name of the game. Terri's preference for natural titties meant that stereotypical stripper types were automatically excluded from the Magic's roster.

There is nothing wrong with getting bigger tits. However it involves a substantial commitment: an emotional and physical investment in a more sexualized body.

I disliked fake breasts because I found them insincere, and if there was one thing I cherished about my new theatrical career, it was its sincerity. Besides that, I was a tomboy and an athlete. I would have paid good money to have my wide hips sawed down to size. But to fill my chest with plastic bags of silicone in an attempt to appear more feminine would have been the ultimate hypocrisy. As a body-obsessed preteen I had petitioned God every morning and night to spare me from sprouting breasts at all!

Certain girls definitely rocked their fake breasts. Not every stripper wants to incorporate sincerity in her act; many are born hams and do well aping the likes of Mae West and Jayne Mansfield. For these girls fake tits are as indispensable as wisecracks. Busty gals also do well with boob jobs, as big busts tend to droop around twenty-five. For them a boob job can extend their career another fifteen years.

Terri didn't give a crap about any of this. She disliked fake boobs almost as much as she disliked independent, intelligent strippers. When Lara Lee got her new tits (turning her overnight into a living, breathing Betty Boop), she found herself off the schedule. When Sophia—who'd been at the Magic for ages and whom Terri loved—got her new breasts, she was relegated to off-nights and morning shifts.

And so the strippers who thrived at Magic were necessarily "different," gals who for one reason or another were not staking their entire identities on careers in stripping, were probably not in it for the long haul, were *au naturel*. This accidental hiring of more down-to-earth girls coupled with an insistence that gals drink and mingle with customers set the Magic apart. Still, the Magic worked in spite of, not because of, Terri.

Terri had a hard time turning the "bad" element out of the Magic: the pimps, bums, and junkies. The other "bad" element—the more creative and self-confident strippers, the lesbians, the organizers and the organized—were easier to get rid of. She just stopped scheduling them. When the girls came in to ask why they weren't getting any shifts, she'd tell them they were too old, too ugly, too lesbian, or too fat. But really they were too independent to allow for Terri's takeover.

I was new and so I was spared. Terri didn't have a read on me until it was too late and I was the press liaison for the local sex industry. But all my friends—the strippers I worshipped and adored like Mona, Morgan, Teresa, and Tommy June—were gone within months.

The Middle

After the bunny omen I started flying alone. I had to—Mona was a train wreck and I wasn't ready to be wrecked alongside her.

She got evicted, dumped her ex-junkie rock-n-roll boyfriend for a photographer with a house and plenty of income and moved in with him. He lived on the other side of town, the bucolic eastern wilds peopled with lesbians with 2.3 children and hippies and garage salers and Reed College students. She might as well have moved to the moon.

Pink was still around, but without Mona's stubborn spark, we both returned to our more natural introspective ways. I woke up early to write in coffee shops and he fussed around in his apartment all day.

I stripped two shifts a week, but that wasn't quite enough to keep me solvent. The winter months tended to be slow; an average shift earned a girl a bit over one hundred dollars. Occasionally the heavens opened and money rained from the sky and I'd walk with two hundred dollars, but that was rare. The Magic wasn't on the map yet; the salad days to come were still only seedlings.

I was forced to take a roommate, and so rented my little "Anne Frank room"—a glorified closet hidden behind a kitchen cupboard—to a hairdresser from Eugene named Eurydice. She lived in a school bus there and owned a salon called the Hairy Truth. She wanted to start expanding to Portland and so came up on weekends to dance a few stripping shifts, where she'd solicit the guys for haircuts, which she performed in my kitchen.

Eurydice was utterly bizarre, a drug-casualty hippie who was deeply in touch with her sexual energy. Onstage she fell into a twitchy trance, jerking around ungracefully and spreading her stuff wide for any guy who could stomach it. She was pixie beautiful—a lovely face heaped with long platinum and brown dreadlocks, a small muscular body, and great tits. She was thirty-eight and looked seventeen. Ahh, drugs. She made a great roommate, being around only several days a month, but on those days I never knew what to expect—which customer would be in my kitchen getting a haircut or if Eurydice would be in the midst of an hour-long tantric orgasm astride her ex-boyfriend on the dirty, painted-black wood floor.

Meanwhile, down at the Magic, various stories competed for prominence regarding Mona's termination, each more unbelievable than the last. Mona herself claimed she'd chucked an ashtray at a guy who was being rude and not tipping. I had thought throwing ashtrays was part of the job. But the victim of Mona's ashtray threatened to sue.

The Magic felt far less magical to me with Mona gone. Unblinded by her otherworldly glow, I started to see the wear on the carpet, the bruises on girls' legs, the missing rhinestones on their G-strings. Stripping became more of a job and less of an all-consuming passion.

Terri, noticing how profitable Mona's cabarets made Sunday nights (though failing to notice her cult of personality), asked Eurydice to continue them. Eurydice's inner Cancer control-freak came out and she soon became Magic's resident dictator, marshalling up all the newbies to dance cheek-to-cheek with customers on Sunday nights. The slow dancing was interspersed with weird acts like her own woodland sprite, wherein she wrapped herself in long fake vines and writhed and whinnied for the duration of an overlong Nina Hagen song.

I politely declined Eurydice's invitation to appear in her shows. Partly it was out of loyalty to Mona, who by then really and truly felt she owned the word *cabaret*—and me along with it. Mo was planning bigger events at concert venues and would disown me or drown me if I performed for anyone else. Mostly, though, I turned down Eurydice's cabarets because they were utterly ridiculous. Don't get me wrong, I'm a huge fan of ridiculous, but coming down after something as sublime as Mona's magical extravaganzas to dance cheek-to-cheek with Magic's resident lonely hearts and then have to suffer through Eurydice's improvised interpretations of sex energy… I couldn't do it. Still it was fun to drop by and see the lowly Magic as a full-on brothel, young beautiful ladies dressed in evening gowns waltzing around with fat/old/lame/loutish guys gussied up in suits on a Sunday night.

My bubble had burst. I really believed in Mona, in her bizarre visions, in her imminent world domination. Now I was just a stripper, and my usual ghosts were coming back to haunt me—the manic dissatisfaction, crippling idealism, stubborn depression, and frantic I-gotta-moves. I thought my fabulous fantasy had come to an abrupt end. Really, though, it was just the end of the beginning.

Check Your Head, Part One

Brand spankin' new naked girl and self-conscious about it? Don't be. You're the cream of the crop when you're new at droppin' trou'. Your innocence, naïveté and excitement as a new girl are completely beguiling to guys. They'll never notice your awkward moves, that you're a little chubby,

The Magic Garden

217 NW 4TH IN HISTORIC CHINATOWN
(503) 224-8472

Cocktail Party JAN 12

DOORS OPEN AT 6PM
DANCE CARDS AVAILABLE FROM 9:30 PM TO 11PM
*Your chance to dance cheek to cheek with your
favorite Magic Garden Girlie!*

★ MISS MONA'S CABARET RETURNS FEBRUARY 9TH ★

OPEN DAILY
12 NOON TO 2 AM
OPEN SUNDAY
AT 6PM

FULL LIQUOR BAR
DAILY LUNCH SPECIAL
KITCHEN OPEN 'TIL 2AM

or that you walk in your stripper heels like a newborn filly. They won't even notice that you've fallen on your naked ass! Your laugh is not yet cynical, it's genuine and generally you're nervous and you giggle a lot. Guys love this. More than they want to look at your divine underpinnings, they want to see you smiling at them. That's why newbies can easily make as much cash as veterans. Frequently they make more.

This honeymoon lasts about three months. It's a heady time for the newbie and she's somewhat vulnerable. When I was a newbie, I found it hard to differentiate between good guys and bad guys. I'd already committed the greatest crime a woman can commit in our society by claiming my right to my own sexuality, so what exactly was "good" and what was "bad"? I had to relearn this over my first few months. Luckily I didn't get killed.

I went out to dinner with strangers. I let a gentleman from Saudi Arabia take me strip club hopping in his giant white limo. I let Black Larry bully me into a shoe buying trip, which made me feel like a triple-whore (not cuz I got "payment" for my favors, but because I let myself be bullied. But more on that later...). I let too many strangers ply me with too much alcohol on unfamiliar beats. I got rides from wasted strippers. I took an all-day motorcycle ride with a customer I'd met twice.

In the last ten years I've seen a hundred strippers learn the ropes the same way. Miraculously we've all lived to see our smiles harden a bit, to rein in our laughter and to say, "No fuckin' way, sir."

The main thing about being a newbie is that you can do no wrong. But you can get killed. And no matter what your mom or your manager says, you'll be vulnerable for three to six months. Unless you're a drug addict or an idiot, in which case it'll be longer.

Drug Addicts

Drugs have their place in the stripper world, but not nearly as much as is generally thought. Strippers are racehorses, after all, and need to take extra good care of their bodies in order to perform. Most are into naturopathic remedies, aromatherapy, yoga, and facials. Many chart moon cycles and know money spells, love potions, and Wicca book-stores. They almost all love pot, sex, and liquor. The drug addicts don't last unless they're really tough. You can recognize them by their emotionless demeanor, opera-length gloves, and thigh-high stockings.

Idiots

The idiot stripper is also uncommon, partly because you get wise quick when you disabuse yourself of society's basic tenet that you should hide your stuff always and thoroughly. Plus any service industry position exposes a person to the diversity of the human race and the ironies and vagaries of human existence. You get wise in spite of yourself on these stages.

Idiot strippers lose track of where the act ends and reality begins. They attract men who value bodies over brains, men who aren't worth a lot of dough as they're easily bored with the same piece of ass. Idiot strippers do stupid things and sometimes disappear. If they come back they are always smarter.

On Disappearances

There was this one guy we called Hundred Dollar Dave. A handsome, well-built man in his late forties, Dave was a graduate of Harvard University and made oodles of money in high tech. He was married to his high school sweetheart and the father of a teenaged daughter and son. He was really fucking crazy and relished humiliating strippers. He made it well worth their while, though, tipping hundreds instead of singles, so many gals would indulge his bizarre mind games, no matter how degrading they appeared.

The thing about humiliation is that YOU make the call whether you feel humiliated or not. It is of utmost importance to know your own boundaries. If you find it humiliating to dance around naked in public, don't do it (but I suggest you reconsider). If you find it humiliating to be ordered to wear your panties backwards in public while bending over in front of a stranger and counting slowly to twenty for a hundred bucks, don't do it (but I suggest you reconsider).

I rebelled at first. "No I will not wear my panties backwards. That's asinine." I would, however, get naked and spread my goods before every guy at the rack, bent over, holding my ankles and counting slowly to twenty. I considered this humiliating and hated doing it. Especially if there was a customer in the bar whom I liked and respected. Still, seeing a hundred dollar bill in place of a single was very persuasive. But bent over in all my gynecological glory—a move I otherwise never embraced—I couldn't help but feel compromised, until one day I had a change of heart. I *decided* that it was NOT humiliating, but rather fun and sorta interesting to indulge in these naughty little head games.

The next time Dave came in, I tried on my G-string backwards in the privacy of the dressing room, only to find that I liked the looks of it. The little triangle of sheer black fabric was in the back, decorating nicely my voluptuous ass, and the thin elastic bisected my little bush like some early eighties fetish fashion. So I wore it onstage and made an easy fifty bucks.

One time when Dave was paying us a visit I had to gently persuade a thousand-dollar roll of hundreds, fifties, and twenties into Claudia's asshole. She got to keep that money, of course, but I worried she might contract hepatitis or something worse—some rare capitalism-induced disease that travels straight to the brain and colonizes it outright. Claudia, however, had no problem with it. And that's why Dave loved her.

Why Dave liked spending thousands of dollars on the degradation of women didn't really interest me. I suspect it was some warped creative outlet for him, coupled with a schizoid love/hate of women. But I always liked it when he came in because it broke the monotony of the shift.

Dave made sure the barmaid was well-compensated so she'd let us bend the rules and play whatever strange game he dreamed up. The rest of the clientele would quickly get freaked out or bored and leave while we girls drank and laughed and spanked each other 'til our asses glowed hot pink, yelping gamely to up the entertainment value.

Not every girl was into it. There was a persistent rumor that Dave offered girls tens of thousands of dollars (and covered hospital bills) to beat the shit out of them in fancy hotel rooms and leave them for dead. A couple reliable sources swore up and down that he'd been held for several days for the Green River murders in Washington. They said he'd only gotten off on a technicality.

I sensed that he was dangerously crazy. I knew by the way his eyes flickered and faded when a gal faked an orgasm or played "Back Door Man" or something by Enigma (his favorite music). He was nuts alright. And probably a killer. But I didn't feel the slightest twinge of guilt at taking his money. The most important thing—as a stripper explained to me the first time I danced for Dave—was to know your own limits and never go beyond them for any amount of money. And never leave with the asshole, either, especially when drunk on vodka tonics or adrenaline from the pain of the tit and clit clamps Dave brought in for us to wear.

But the girls Dave was most fond of seemed to be the ones who hadn't thought of limits—girls who aimed to please and would do just about anything if asked. Claudia—the cat with one thousand bucks up her ass—was that kind of girl.

For a while Dave came in every time Claudia worked. He'd motion me to his seat where a drink would be waiting for me. Then he'd whisper, "I want you to take Claudia in the dressing room and spank her pussy until she begs for mercy. Tell her she's been very naughty and deserves it."

I must have spanked her several hundred times. She never once wanted me to fake it. Most "slaves" giggled and played along as you clapped your hands together or slapped your thigh with the leather whips and paddles Dave supplied for us, but not Claudia. She wanted you to actually get your hands dirty. She wanted you to spank her so hard the welts would show even under the red lights.

Dave's favorite humiliation for Claudia was to have her stand at the bar bent-over with her head buried in her arms, naked below the waist. Often times the club would be busy when he requested this. It was very disconcerting and somewhat heartbreaking to see it, even if you knew what kind of money she was making.

Claudia had no boundaries. She even left with Dave now and then and when she wouldn't show up for work we'd assume the worst. But soon enough she'd reappear with some absent-minded excuse that reeked of marijuana.

Eventually she took the money and ran, all the way to India and Ethiopia in search of Jah. She married an Ethiopian and came back crazier than ever. Last I heard she'd been born again and was studying massage in Hawaii.

Willamette Week

I was getting pretty comfortable in my dancing shoes.

I loved my job and my job loved me. I worked two five-hour shifts a week. The rest of the time I scribbled religiously in coffee shops, writing manifesto-like letters to college pals and professors and filling journals with the magical details of my wondrous and inspiring new milieu. At night I'd bike around listening to bands and dreaming of having my own. In the meantime I survived on hummus and beer at Fellini, the rocker hangout next to Satyricon, an infamous club on gritty 6th Avenue. I loved being a stripper, loved the cowgirl identity of having no one to answer to, galloping around the Wild West, independent and free. I loved heading to work on my bike with my huge duffel bag, riding down Everett Street in the midst of traffic, stopping for a shot at Fellini, all made up for battle and buzzing like a pretty bee. I loved watching my co-workers take it off, losing myself in the curve of a back, the beat of a song, the reflections of humanity. And I loved stripping. I loved talking about stripping, loved arguing about stripping, loved championing its cause. I truly believed that stripping was art, and I rejoiced that I'd found my niche.

Mona and Teresa had different philosophies. Teresa's party line was that stripping was a job. Therefore, strippers should be respected as workers and accorded basic worker's rights, like on-the-job access to health and safety supplies. Teresa didn't have time to talk right or

WILLAMETTE

VUE 19 | MARCH 12, 1997 | PORTLAND NEWS AND CULTURE

WEEK

PORN

Two Views

PAGE 20

wrong. She said, *"Where are the rubber gloves, the bleach, the first aid kit, the bio-hazard disposal containers?"*

To tell Mona that any kind of human behavior was wrong was like talking to a brick wall. If animals are going to rape and murder, love and hate, cheat and steal, so be it. Mo saw the bullshit inherent in civilization from birth. You could sooner reconcile the Palestinians and Israelis than stop Miss Mona from doing exactly as she pleased. She was a force of nature. Tell a hurricane to go away. Tell a flood to skip your basement. To Mona, stripping was stripping. Not good, not bad, just a means to an end. Try telling her otherwise and you were likely to get an ashtray in the head.

Me, I was all peace, love, and understanding. The naked way was the only way! Provocatively normal, abundantly life-affirming. I felt confident people would see this eventually, if only I could show them. I was a preacher's kid; preaching was in my bones. When I believed in something, I became evangelical. I hadn't believed in much of anything in a while.

I believed that stripping was art. At the strip clubs, I was preaching to the choir.

Enter Jill Portugal.

Jill was in her mid-twenties, a graduate of Brown, a somewhat spoiled and sheltered girl who held the indulgent belief that if a stranger admired your body they were uninterested in your mind. (They're STRANGERS! Praise Jesus they notice anything at all. Most folks are blind, deaf, and dumb to anything outside of their cell phones.) Provoked by an off-color cartoon by off-color cartoonist John Callahan, she penned a letter to the popular local weekly, *Willamette Week*.

To Whom It May Concern,

The Callahan cartoon in the Dec. 4 issue confused me. Was the cartoonist urging that feminists be killed and stuffed into mailboxes, as the illustration showed, or was he suggesting that feminism is dead? So I stared at it for a while, trying to understand what was funny about it. But nothing was.

I guess it doesn't much matter what the great Callahan intended, since either interpretation amounts to the same thing for me: Oregon doesn't exactly have a female-friendly climate, and feminism's pretty comatose here.

Plus, it's not the first time Willamette Week *has blithely printed*

*something obnoxious and offensive to its female readership. Over the sum-
mer, in their "Best of Portland" issue, the editors saw fit to publish some quasi-
pornographic paragraphs under the heading "Best Nude Dancer." The entry
explained the award-winning technique of a local stripper in comprehensive
detail. I understand* WW *prides itself on its "irreverent" and "edgy" news.
Oh, how very playful to write about strippers. How wonderfully cutting-
edge to describe naked women in print. Oh, what a naughty little newspaper
you are!*

*This is what I hate about Portland: exploitation disguised as innova-
tion, degradation parading as freedom. For me, there's nothing very freeing
about living in a state whose consumer-to-porn ratio ranks the highest in the
nation. There's nothing particularly liberating about being in a place where
adult bookstores can set up shop next to schools, so boys can get a jump start
on porn consuming. There's nothing enjoyable about walking down the street
and waiting for the bus next to a newspaper vending machine selling naked women to anyone with two quarters, right next to a machine that sells*
USA Today. *And there's nothing especially wonderful about riding past a
strip joint on the highway that boasts* LIVE NUDE GIRLS *in huge red letters, the same way supermarkets advertise* GREEN BEANS 79 CENTS A
POUND.

*As you might guess, I abhor the porn industry with violent intensity.
Because it exploits and hurts women. Because I believe it's fundamentally
impossible both to consume porn, and to respect women as people. And because
Portland is so steeped in porn culture, I know I can't stay here.*

*In New York, where I'm from, porn theaters and shops are zoned off
into one seedy district where drug dealers hang out. Porn use is slightly stig-
matized and nothing you'd readily admit to. But here in Oregon, I see that
porn's been thoroughly mainstreamed and rendered remarkably accessible,
and watching strippers is just another entertainment option. It's an accept-
able evening activity—should we go bowling, rent a movie, or pay to look at
naked girls tonight? Even worse, it's become a viable career choice for women.
These things do not make for a female-friendly climate, nor a safe one. Living in a city where porn is sold out of vending machines on street corners is
fucked.*

*At this point people usually cut me off by saying, it's the woman's choice and
all that. Not much of a choice when the sex industry pays three or four times the
rate of a job that any ordinary Oregon woman could do with her clothes on. It's*

not about "art" or "feminine power," as some would claim. It's about cash and the sale of naked women. Tell me, ladies, would you dance around naked for my wage, $6.50 an hour? Would you do it for minimum wage?

Everyone wants to make a nice living, but please understand that your choices affect others. If you strip for cash, you help feed Oregon's porn culture, which means that overall women cannot be respected as people here, which leads to my getting harassed on the street by men I don't know. Which means I can't walk down to Burnside at night to return a video without four different guys giving me shit about my face or hair or body. They don't care whether I'm a preschool teacher or a prostitute—to them I'm just nice scenery.

At this point people usually cut me off and talk about free speech. So great, I've got the freedom to publish trash on the World Wide Web. That's supercool and real consoling to me as I'm waiting for a cab to take me home from a concert because it's not safe for women to walk alone at night. All the free speech in the world won't make women safe. I'd trade some of my so-called freedoms if you could make me feel safe. But that's a freedom I'll never have.

I can see all the things I've written about as an interconnected chain of phenomena, because I've been thinking about this stuff for five years. And after five years, one's opinions are unshakable, so please don't waste ink or breath arguing with me.

[Jill Portugal
Willamette Week 1/22/97
Letters, "Reviving Feminism"]

I read the letter over coffee and a scone at Umbra. Soon I was shaking all over, my heart pumping adrenaline to every extremity. I was pissed, sure, but mostly I was thrilled. Here was an invitation, an open door. The gauntlet had been thrown. I reread the letter with my pen, underlining with fervor and making notes in the margins: What did she mean by feminism anyway? If feminism didn't allow sex workers into its ranks, then it should be dead. Was naked dancing so reprehensible an occupation that a local gal shouldn't be honored with "Best Nude Dancer?" Were *USA Today*'s portrayals of women so much rosier than *Exotic Magazine*'s, in which self-employed women flashed their privates and a smile?

Finally it was time to put my mouth where my money was and preach to a bigger flock. Everyone from punk rockers to politicians read the *Willamette Week*. If I could show them just a little bit of what I loved about my work, give them a peek at an industry that most people preferred be invisible, it'd be a huge coup for my crew.

I worked hard on my response at the little hippie coffee shop above Jazz de Opus on 2nd Avenue. I chose my words carefully, typed them up at Kinko's, then hand-delivered my letter to the weekly's offices.

Dear Jill Portugal,

I'd rather not dignify your puritanical self-righteous misogynistic opinions with a response, as you suggested, but HELL you put them into the public forum where they did sufficiently enrage me and mine, so here goes…

1. *MONEY IS POWER*

   If you choose to prostitute yourself to capitalism for $6.50 an hour, that is your business. My time is worth more. A hell of a lot more. So I get naked for $40 an hour. Still not enough (what is?), but at least my creativity, intelligence, and effervescent wit are more highly appreciated than they would be doing data entry for a pittance.

2. *MONEY IS POWER!*

   Where is the $6.50 you earn coming from? Which environments and/or nations and/or peoples are being economically and spiritually raped and plundered to profit the man who doles out your righteous wage? I believe, perhaps naively, that the dollar bills I earn are more honest than that. I know where they are coming from and why. Taking five hours out of my day to dance to rock 'n' roll sans apparel is worth approximately $200 to me. Capitalism, straight up. I'm not thrilled about working for the man, so I've found a way to do it as little as possible.

3. *MONEY IS POWER!!*

   The first feminists were sex industry workers. Often referred to by the ironic misnomer "prostitutes," these women traded sex for money and thereby became self-sufficient from the man. Even today women caught in patriarchal situations can find escape through this tried and true route, be it in tribal Africa, urban Asia, or right here in the U.S. To me, this sounds more like empowerment than "degradation." Consider: it was once thought a violation of woman's purity and her sacred feminine nature that she work outside the home or vote. Call Off Your Old Tired Ethics!

4. *NAKED BODIES ARE BEAUTIFUL*
    This is one of the few beliefs cherished across cultures and time. Why not own up? Places where naked bodies are subverted and nudity considered degrading are precisely those wherein women's rights and other freedoms are the most in jeopardy. I would advise you to examine the misogynistic opinions you may have been unconsciously inculcated with in this admittedly inimical society. Misogyny is much more than skin deep.

5. *I AM SORRY YOU GET HARASSED ON THE STREET*
    We all do. But you only become the victim when you call it that. Have you ever been to a strip club? You might find that you are in fact more highly respected and celebrated in one of Portland's deplorable titty bars than at your degrading ($6.50 an hour?!?) job.

6. USA TODAY *IS FAR MORE MISOGYNISTIC THAN* EXOTIC MAGAZINE
    - *Is your precious human soul more offended by seeing its body cut up and stuffed with bullets or in a T-back and pasties?*
    - *Which of these periodicals is devoted to and primarily paid for by self-employed women?*
    - *Which has a higher female-to-male writer ratio?*

Jill, my definition of a feminist is a free-thinking woman (or man). According to this definition, there is room for both of us in the movement. There is not, however, room for misogynistic thinking in a fight against misogyny. Unlike yours, my opinions are not set-in-stone, and I hope they never will be. Because I am confident that my free-thinking feminism could only benefit from some discourse, I'd like to invite you out for coffee. Your choice—the safe, PC world of Northwest 23rd or the sin city of Northwest 4th. I frequent both, but if you want to find me, I call the Magic Gardens home. Best titty bar in town. Northwest 4th and Everett.

[Viva Las Vegas
Willamette Week, 3/5/97
Letters, "What Is Feminism, Anyway?"]

Several days later, in the midst of a dull day shift at the Magic, the phone rang. It was *Willamette Week* asking for Viva Las Vegas. The barkeep squealed with excitement as I took the phone.

Would I be willing to meet Jill Portugal in their office, with a tape recorder, for a debate? I tried to sound blasé, said Oh-sure-why-not, but again my adrenaline surged. This could be a coup d'état.

I prepared meticulously for our meeting, dusted off Foucault, read new sex texts in the coffee shop at Powell's Books, and made detailed notes of points I wanted to bring up, knowing full well that in the heat of the moment my temper might get away from me.

The day of the debate arrived. I dressed carefully, choosing what I felt was representative of me and of the sophisticated yet anarchic strip scene I loved: black wool turtleneck, Levi's 501s, motorcycle boots, bleach blonde hair, and dark red lipstick. I screwed on some vintage ruby and rhinestone earrings to add a smidgen of glamour. Then I pedaled my ass to SW 10th Avenue, giving myself a pep talk on the way.

I had tried to anticipate what it would be like, figured Jill would be catty and dogmatic and that we'd have a strongman present to separate us and a docile lady reporter egging us on. It was sort of like that, except the newsweekly evidently thought every male staff member would be required to restrain us. Or, more likely, they wanted to see the show.

I do better performing in front of crowds, especially when the high and mighty are present, and here they were. Both of the paper's founders sat at the long office table, along with a bunch of reporters. One fellow looked vaguely Midwestern and was wearing a wedding ring. I instinctively moved to chat him up, hoping to make the situation less intimidating and more human, a trick I'd learned at the strip club.

"Pardon me, sir, but are you from the Midwest?"

He looked a little taken aback. "I was born and raised in South Dakota, though I haven't been back for years."

"I knew it! You look a bit like my dad. All my people are from South Dakota."

Voilà, the ice was broken, the room had thawed. Except for Jill Portugal, who sat across from me, snarling.

"You must be Jill," I said warmly. "Nice to meet you."

She shook my hand disdainfully, as if it were disagreeable for her to even touch me. She wore the usual post-collegiate Gap gear: elegant brown jeans and a snug brown t-shirt, little makeup and shoulder-length curly brown hair. I wouldn't catcall her, but it was conceivable that others would.

The group was called to order by the editor-in-chief. I flipped through my handwritten notes, trying to focus my head and calm my stomach, but to no avail.

"Don't be nervous," the lady reporter said calmly. "We'll make this as quick and painless as possible."

"It just feels weird to be wearing so many clothes in front of such a big crowd," I quipped. The assembly laughed politely and the tape recorders clicked on.

For ninety minutes we engaged in polite debate. Portugal, à la Women's Studies 101, focused more on her personal background than on the world around her. I tried to dodge that, but the reporters wanted dirt. What did my preacher father think about my new career? How did I feel about my mom? I sensed the trajectory of the article from the questions, and tried to calmly throw in the points I felt I needed to make—the Teresa/Viva/Mona points: stripping is a job, stripping is art, stripping is stripping.

After the debate Jill and I were led into the hallway—all the pee-ons lined up with their tongues on the floor—for a photo shoot. I reapplied my "Vixen" lipstick and punked my platinum hair. Jill didn't want to be photographed, but consented to being scenery— her arms sternly crossed across her ample bosom. I smirked for the camera, then hopped on the back of my bike and rode like a bat out of hell to Fellini.

I was sure they were gonna make an ass out of me. It would be difficult not to, considering some of the asinine questions I'd been asked. I ordered some whiskey, the bar bought me a beer, a cute boy appeared, and I gave him my address.

I got tipsy and biked home. I changed into a black velvet pantsuit and, rubber bands around my ankles, biked in the rain to the Keller Auditorium where I saw *The Magic Flute* for the fifth time. And wept. Afterward I visited Pink at the porn store and went back to Fellini for more whiskey. My destiny was again in someone else's hands. I could drink.

Several long weeks passed and the *Willamette Week* still hadn't run my letter to the editor. I worried they wouldn't, would instead skip straight to the debate and my carefully plotted diatribe would be subsumed by the prurient catfight. Whatever. Maybe they wouldn't run it at all.

I drank a lot. The cute boy with the address all but moved in. He drank a lot, too.

Finally, in early March, they printed the letter. It was a knockout. Nothing more to be said, I felt. I was so proud. My heroes were proud of me, too.

Then, a week later, the debate ran. Cover story.

Fame

One reason I like stripping is because I'm shy yet still have an insatiable ego. Most actors act for this reason, I imagine. You gotta have an outlet.

Onstage I was larger than life; I was wildfire. I could maintain it for five or six hours, then I'd collapse from exhaustion. I'd resume my street urchin shtick and slink around on my bike, observing the worker ants and trying my darndest to be invisible.

When the *Willamette Week* put me on its cover, my smirking face staring from every corner coin box, every coffee shop, every bus stop, I was a fox on the run. It seemed to me I'd never seen so many people actually engrossed in any one periodical. Everyone everywhere was reading it, their heads buried between my face and a bunch of back page ads for busty girls and herpes support groups.

It wasn't quite the brutal press rape I had feared. I was mortified to read that I had "burst into tears" while talking about my parents (I remembered getting misty-eyed, but in no way "bursting") and was quite offended by several sloppy misquotes, but for the most part I felt that the salient points had made it into print and that both sides were treated fairly. I came across as intelligent, polite, and rather spoiled. Portugal came across as impulsive, whiny, and rather spoiled.

I went to a lot of movies to hide out during the daylight hours. At night I hung out at Fellini and apologized to my peers for being so mercenary and egotistical as to allow my countenance to be splashed across a yuppie fish wrapper. After all I am from Minnesota. Minnesotans champion humility over all other virtues. Minnesotans are embarrassed to be alive.

I figured the article was entirely forgettable. It wasn't. For the next six weeks the *Willamette Week* ran impassioned letters to the editor, most picking on Jill for her holier-than-thou paralyzing liberal feminism. A few criticized my choices, my naïveté, and my romantic worldview. Every week between one and five letters ran. The weekly had never had such a response.

At the Magic I became a minor celebrity, to my dismay. All my friends were getting axed, usually for getting too big for their britches. Lara Lee had been voted Best Stripper in Portland by the *Willy Week* and promptly got the boot. Mona was thrown to the dogs when her star took off, too. Even Teresa was just too ambitious and smart to take a chance on. I was sure I was next. For the next eight years.

If Magic's management was a wild card, its customers were not. Men and women called to find out when I was working and came in to shake my hand. One penguin in a really nice suit stopped by over lunch with his briefcase, handed me a twenty, said "thank you," and left. For months and even years afterward, people would recognize me as "that girl from the *Willamette Week*." Even in Boston and New York City. It amazed me that so many folks found this silly debate of a nonissue (nudity is alright; sex is okay) as fascinatingly hypocritical—and worthy of critical thought—as I did. I felt like I could talk about it forever; sensed I just might have found my life's calling.

The goals Mom and Dad thought were a fatal waste of time—to have fun fighting a losing battle, to be stubbornly aware of hypocrisy every goddamned day, no matter how exhausting and sad and hopeless—had been deemed worthy.

Carnal Carnival

Strippers are an itinerant race. The polar opposite of wage slaves, we are hunter-gatherers. Certain things will ground a girl—a hearty drug habit, a shopping fetish, or a child—but most of us come and go like the seasons.

At Magic, Zyola came and went in my first six months. She'd stripped for her first time two months after my debut, turning me suddenly from baby bird to old pro, although we were exactly the same age.

Zyola had a luxuriously curvy body and creamy white skin. Naked she looked like a well-dressed bed, beckoning with overstuffed pillows. The black guys loved her, and she happily shook her shit for them. She'd grind her large white ass on the rail, do the butt dance for entire songs, and stare at men hungrily with her big green eyes. She was an excellent stripper, if a so-so dancer. She knew her audience and made sure they got what they came in for.

Zyola had only been dancing for three or four months when she fell in love with a shy man at the bar. Within days she'd traded her stage time for cocktailing shifts and was soon pregnant.

It shocked me to see girls go. I'd moved a dozen times before I landed in Portland; I was accustomed to being the one who left, who moved on. The Magic was my family, and the fact that girls just up and left made me queasy. I loved them! It was like having your favorite socks walk out on you.

Mona had been fired. So had Teresa, Morgan, and June. Even Rose, the finger-banger, left abruptly. Rumor was she'd been fired for soliciting. I was sad to see her go. I looked up to these girls, worshipped them even.

Of course new girls trickled in to take their places. The job seemed to appeal most to freelancers: gals who taught yoga, volunteered for the public good, were students or prostitutes. I swear working forty hours a week for one entity is a deadly waste of any human's myriad talents, and I've no doubt God gets disappointed.

New girls started out on the noon to four shift. If an audition was especially fabulous, Terri would schedule the girl for a mid-shift so she

Miss Mona's **CARNAL CARNIVAL**

★ THE SEXIEST SHOW ON EARTH ★

SUNDAY APRIL 6TH

BERBATI'S PAN

$6 AT THE DOOR ★ 231 SW ANKENY ★ 248-4579

Dr. Ducky Doolittle

Quasi

Ernest Truely

ONE SHOW ONLY
7 PM COME EARLY! STAY LATE!

could get a good look at her and see how she went over with the customers. Terri was always eager to lock down the busy Friday and Saturday night shifts with an extra-exotic bird. Rain, the reigning queen of the Magic, was after all only one person, and she had the bad habit of getting so wasted she'd pass out before the end of her shift.

Echo and Celeste started around this time. They were hippie chicks, thin tawny gals with soft downy armpit hair, unshaved pussies, and serious demeanors. Echo was short and wiry; her wispy shoulder-length hair twisted into ringlets and she wore little-to-no makeup. She looked like the girl-next-door's little sister. Celeste was more celestial. Waves of blonde hair cascaded halfway down her back. She had the longest, thinnest, loveliest legs ever seen outside a horse track. Celeste moved extremely slowly and gracefully, the kind of striptease I liked best. The hem of her short diaphanous flowered slip just barely allowed a peek at her pussy. It wasn't long before Celeste was dancing every Saturday night. Echo remained stuck on day shifts. The Magic was the perfect place for them to make cash while awaiting trial. They'd both been arrested for felony trespassing that winter when they climbed aboard a large oil tanker as part of a Greenpeace operation.

Meanwhile Teresa, Morgan, and Tommy June had all picked up shifts at Mary's Club, another strip dive down the street. I was working my ass off at Magic while fielding phone calls to pose for photos, be sketched for paintings, play the leads in independent films. The *Willamette Week* article seemed to have inspired lots of different folks, and I felt beholden to them as muse.

My day planner was filled with meetings with artists, guitarists, writers, and filmmakers. There was only occasionally money involved, and if there was, I'd get suspicious and run away. I helped on as many projects as I could—my own nonprofit adjunct of Mona's cabarets and Teresa's *Danzine*. We were spreading the good news, fighting the good fight. I could barely pay my rent but that didn't matter; I was young and excited and could run on fumes indefinitely.

Mo was hard at work preparing for our cabaret's debut at Berbati's, a large rock club with a fabulously huge stage. She was fielding lots of phone calls, too. South by Southwest wanted to host our troupe, ad agencies asked us to perform at their parties to up their hipster cachet, newspapers had to have interviews, the public demanded photos, even art galleries came knocking. But Mona wasn't as willing as I was to be eaten alive. She cloistered herself in her cottage on Liebe Street (in between Goethe and Schiller Streets) and smoked pounds of pot, pen and paper in hand.

Only the best of Mona's cabaret crew were invited to perform Miss Mona's Carnal Carnival. We had enough of a reputation now to recruit new gals from the larger, more prissy clubs across town. Even they were eager to toss off their G-strings for the cause.

Mona called a meeting at my Lawn apartment. She distributed fat packets of cabaret history and legend, required reading with blurbs on Josephine Baker, Lili St. Cyr, Tempest Storm, Sally Rand (named after the Rand McNally Atlas, don't ya know) and more, filled with photos and topped off with nine pages of the comic *Weird Burlesque* by Stephen Holman. Mona had to make sure we all knew what was expected of us. This was no sex kitten show, this was weird burlesque.

She lectured us all on dates and times. No stripper bullshit would fly for this show. You missed a rehearsal, you were out. She'd also hand-picked everyone's music and all but blocked their entire acts. We'd hit the big time and Mona was hungry—so hungry she'd chewed her fingernails halfway down to the quick.

"Viva! You are going to dress up as a cowgirl and sing 'Stand By Your Man' to a dog. Can you play 'Stand By Your Man' on guitar? No? LEARN IT!"

I bought a Tammy Wynette compilation and scribbled down the lyrics. The guitar part was easy enough. I practiced and practiced in front of a mirror on my Grandma's old classical guitar.

Mona had formed a Portland all-star band to back us up, the Fon-Dells. Louie, a tattooed suave from the Flapjacks, was recruited to play drums. Sten, who rarely appeared before dark and never without his sunglasses, played guitar. He was a local legend and was currently playing in the Oblivion Seekers and the Lucky Thirteens. A lady saxophonist from god-knows-where signed on, too, and blew the fuck out of the old stripper anthems like "Night Train" as well as "Stand By Your Man." Yvan, the darling young hipster bass player from the Weaklings, rounded out the band.

We rehearsed the tune twice in the basement of Louie's house tucked into the industrial wasteland on the east side of the river. For me it was a dream come true—Marilyn Monroe singing Tammy Wynette fronting the hottest band-for-hire in town! Veteran rockers led by a pipsqueak upstart. I thanked my lucky stars yet again.

For days I combed thrift stores for cheap cowboy boots and big ol' silver belt buckles. I found a child's peach ultra-suede vest, edged with fringe and emblazoned with musical notes and a bass and a treble clef, all in glitter and glue gun. Perfect! I found a matching fringe bra for $1.99 at Fantasy Video on Burnside and got a kid's cowboy hat and little pistols with holsters from Toy-R-Us. The dog somebody else procured: a deaf Jack Russell terrier.

Sandwiched between shopping trips and stripping shifts was a lunch meeting with Mark Zusman, the very handsome forty-something cofounder and editor-in-chief of *Willamette Week*. He was a big wig locally, and when I breezed right past the weekly's front desk and into his office, the cubicle kids wet themselves, utterly confounded.

Mark was progressive politically and loved to help us proactive strippers in any way he could. Generally this meant free advertising, but after my *WW* interview, I had joked that maybe "Zussy" could give me some "career counseling."

In spite of my growing confidence, I was beginning to be plagued by *the shoulds*; I had been out of college almost a year, my loans would soon go into repayment, I could barely afford the minimum on my maxed credit card, I had no health insurance, and my parents were sorely disappointed. I didn't even have a band, the whole reason I'd come to Portland, and all my coffee shop scribblings seemed to amount to nothing. Could it be true that my glamorous new career was indeed the dead end everyone said it was?

Mark and I talked for an hour about all and sundry at the little lunch counter next to Finnegan's toy store on 10th Avenue. When I'm up against a nine-to-fiver, I get defensive about my irascible and possibly irreversible life choices. But Mark wasn't there to fight. He seemed to think what I was doing was just fine—respectable and even admirable. I was only twenty-two, after all. There was no imperative—even amongst the Williams crowd—to fall in line and buy a suit just because I wouldn't have health insurance or a retirement plan by twenty-three. If Mark Zusman thought it was alright, then I was alright with it, too.

Two days later Miss Mona's Carnal Carnival lit up the night sky. When Viva Las Vegas was announced, the sold-out crowd screamed and chanted "VIVA! VIVA!" I shook in Mona's two-sizes-too-big white cowboy boots as I sauntered onstage with Grandma's guitar, where the little deaf dog was waiting. I adjusted the microphone and pitched one leg up on the dog's velvet chair. I tentatively plucked a *G* chord to kick off the song, but my fingers were shaking too badly. I considered bolting offstage but instead giggled into the microphone. The crowd went wild. Alright so they were easy to please. I swallowed hard and picked apart the *G* chord anew.

"Sometimes it's hard to be a woman…"

I warbled thinly into the microphone, nervous and breathy. At the chorus, the band kicked in. And so did I.

"STAND BY YOUR MAN!"

I belted it out, wringing every bit of pathos from the sad song. The dog just sat there in front of the packed house, beaming beatifically. Having the band behind me gave me such strength, such power. When the song was over, the crowd screamed "Viva!" and "Encore!" The *Willamette Week* article had, it seemed to me, made this Viva Las Vegas character public provenance. Fine, I thought. They needed her more than I did.

Later that week the *WW* published a big review of the show in their Culture section, daring considering we were all a bunch of strippers. In it they singled out my "rousing rendition of 'Stand By Your Man'" and "Mona herself, slinking around in a slit-to-the-waist satin gown and seven-inch heels." It even quoted one of the show's MCs:

"Ladies, you don't have to show your genitals to put on a good show, but it sure doesn't hurt."

Johnny Angel

There are two questions I always get asked about stripping.

What do you do when you're on your period?

Does stripping have any effect on your intimate relationships?

The first question is far and away the most common. Everyone from my über-intellectual college gal-pals to my goofy brother and his Army chums wants to know.

What do they think? We take a week off? I've seen strippers dance with food poisoning, pneumonia, herpes, all-over road rash from a bike accident, a broken ankle… Getting your period is a cakewalk. You simply grab a tampon, cut the string, then shove it where the sun don't shine. (Almost every girl has started bleeding onstage at one time or other. Although she's generally mortified, I like to think it increases her exoticism. If it ever happens to me I intend to say to the boys, "Looks like it's your lucky day!")

Now for the second question: Does stripping affect my intimate relationships? Which is the part I don't want to tell you, the part about Johnny Angel.

* * *

Johnny Angel and I met at Fellini, the café-bar next to the Satyricon. I was drunk; I had just sat for the *Willamette Week* debate and was trying to tame my nerves. He was incredibly handsome: tall and lean, with dark curly hair and penetrating green eyes and a rebellious stance that made him a ringer for James Dean.

"Are you gay or just gorgeous?" I quipped, my standard line.

His upper lip curled into a snarl. Or maybe it was a smile.

"You have a girlfriend, don't you?" His reticence clued me in.

"Maybe," he said, snottily.

"Too bad. You're pretty damn cute."

"Can I have your phone number?"

He had balls, at least.

"No way." I snickered.

"Please?"

"No. 'Cause then you'll keep calling and calling and I'll have to get my number changed. I've been there already."

I grabbed the cocktail napkin from under his beer and scribbled my address on it with a Sharpie from the bar. I signed it *VIVA*, with a big anarchy *A* dotting the *I*.

"Here." I shoved it into his hand. "Stop by when you don't have a girlfriend."

The next night Johnny Angel knocked on my door. It was 3 AM. I plugged in the Christmas lights that led to the playroom and slipped into my kimono. I peered through the peephole and thought twice about letting him in. What the hell.

"You single already?" I asked.

"Yeah, well, I was just sorta in the neighborhood, figured I'd stop by."

I handed him a beer and grabbed one for myself.

"Well, sit down. Stay a while."

He stayed. For five years.

For five years I played the girlfriend: brunch every Sunday, in-laws every Christmas, champagne breakfasts in the yard, birthday bashes for the cats. Johnny was an absolute angel: he carried my stripper bag, hauled my guitars and amps, cooked elaborate meals, always did the dishes and took out the trash. He rubbed my sore stripper feet every morning while he read the *New York Times* to me in bed. He bought me expensive shoes. He was well-groomed and worked hard. And we had loads in common: we were both writers, both rockers. In short, he was the perfect boyfriend. But I couldn't let myself love him. Love was a liability, after all. It'd all but sunk me after high school, something my senior yearbook presaged when I summed up my experience with a quote attributed to Plato, "Love is a grave mental disease."

I never intended to stay in Portland more than two years; the world was much too big. A casual affair seemed advisable. The last thing on my to-do list was domestic bliss, even though it soon became clear that Johnny wanted to make me a yuppie wife. Of course that wasn't in the cards. But I'm a damn good actress, and managed to stomach the role for five years. I am practiced at maintaining façades and creating defenses.

It wasn't stripping that made me so remote, so defended. I acquired those skills long ago, during my Midwestern childhood, moving every couple of years to a new town where Dad had a church. I think part of the reason stripping so appeals to me is because it allows me to play at intimacy.

Most strippers have boyfriends. Most are in long-term relationships. Contrary to popular belief, we are not all nymphomaniac she-vixens intent on marrying the fattest wallet that walks through the door. That's just a role we come to master, a role expected of us. But when 3 AM rolls around, we'd rather peel off the glitter and Lycra and lay down next to someone we know and love. Most strippers probably even have enough confidence and emotional depth to peel off the everything's-groovy stripper mask, let down their guard, and CONNECT with their partners. But not me.

For five years he doted on me, doglike in his love and loyalty. The most I managed to give back was a strange demon hybrid of love poisoned with animosity and resentment. I tried, too, to sever our ties, but I wasn't strong enough. Finally, after faking it for so long, I began to lose track of myself, unsure which of my actions were true and which were false. But I was sure that if I stayed with Johnny Angel, I'd jump off a bridge.

Beautiful angel Johnny. Oftentimes I wished with all my heart that our relationship would work, that I'd lose my perverted allegiance to some superhero destiny I'd convinced myself of, magically fall in love with him, and have my feet rubbed for all eternity. But it just doesn't work like that, does it? The heart won't be forced into anything against its will, no matter how advisable.

One gorgeous May afternoon in Pisa, Italy, after more than four years attached at the hip, I unceremoniously dumped him. I told him I'd never loved him. He was stunned and threatened to throw himself in the Arno. We returned to Florence and kept up our role-playing for one more week in Venice and Paris. Then, on the platform of the A train at the Fulton Street subway station in Brooklyn, I bid my angel adieu.

So, how does stripping affect my intimate relationships? At one time I would have said, "Not at all." Now, after nine years, I'd say, "What intimate relationships?"

Back to School: Stripping is Art

That stripping can be art is, I think, a no-brainer. That the mere statement of this is provocative only serves to legitimize it, and, naturally, to provoke me.

Shortly after the debate ran in the *Willamette Week,* I received a letter from a Portland State University professor, care of the Magic Gardens. Would I be interested in addressing her philosophy of aesthetics course on my favorite topic? Hell yes I would.

I devoured their textbook, *Basic Issues in Aesthetics,* and again found myself spending afternoons in Powell's Books, brushing up on my competition (Dworkin, who equates porn with rape), my Foucault (who maintains that society's discursive obsession with sex is no different than a physical obsession with sex), and my porn. Once again I made detailed notes because I knew I'd be nervous. The classroom always intimidated me; the peculiar stage presence required eludes me utterly.

I mulled over some tough nuggets: What happens when people respond aesthetically? Is a hard-on indicative of an aesthetic experience? If the viewer sees art but the doer does not consciously create art, is it art? If the doer is consciously creating art and the viewer doesn't get it, is it art? What is art?

Was stripping always art? It was certainly always an aesthetic experience. What was its value as such? How was a stripper different from a ballerina, a nude model in a painting, a Shakespearean soliloquy? I believed stripping was more honest, unscripted and in the moment. Did that negate its being art? How was "art" different from "artifact?" A stripper's body was not her creation, was more artifact. Her stripping— her active involvement, her commentary and manipulation—was the work of art. Yet still it was frequently unscripted. Must art be scripted, carefully planned, no longer open to chaos, no longer morphing? Must it be static? Finished?

Finally, ought morality have any bearing on what is art? If stripping were not peripheral, were more accepted, would it still be—to my mind—art? Could art be influenced by context and society? Of course it could: at the time of their conception, Degas' ballerinas were considered prurient and scandalous and paintings like Manet's "Olympia" were kept behind velvet curtains and seen only at stag parties. Similarly, Americans might feel that stripping was a beyond-the-pale morally reprehensible choice, whereas people from Amsterdam or Afghanistan would see a different picture altogether.

Marcia M. Eaton, in *Basic Issues in Aesthetics,* defines art thusly: "*X* is a work of art if and only if *x* is an artifact and *x* is discussed in such a way that information concerning its history of production brings the audience to attend to intrinsic properties considered worthy of attention in aesthetic traditions (history, criticism, theory)."

I prefer to ask, *Does it move you?*

My resultant definition of the motherfucker, after much hair-pulling and espresso consumption: ART IS a creation that is an expression of an individual's understanding of existence, with an eye towards engaging and communicating with the public (through harmony/disharmony of sounds, colors, plots, forms, etc.).

The way I saw it, stripping was art because it was self-expression and beauty through movement. It was a sociologically charged interaction with an audience. And it was undoubtedly an aesthetic experience. So what if people found stripping to be tacky, blue-collar, uneducated, uninformed, and even dangerous? There was no denying it was provocative, beautiful, and subversive.

Eaton claims there is a "Goal of Art," which is to "unite people in feelings of communing with one another." She also feels there is such a thing as inherent aesthetic value: "Aesthetic value is freed of any dependence upon the (good or bad) consequences it has in other areas of human experience... Aesthetic experience is not valuable just because it is pleasurable; it is valuable because people who partake of it become more sensitive, more imaginative."

So, was a hard-on indicative of an aesthetic experience? What about a whole bar full of them? One way or another, the audience was moved. Ultimately, art—like stripping—lingers with you, grows into something bigger, something other, seasons the soul.

* * *

My lecture occurred at a long table filled with twenty eager students aged twenty-two to forty-five. I was probably the youngest person in the room, and my insides quivered like Jell-O, but I snapped into character when I was given the floor. I talked about my personal history and my background in art and sociology, then waxed passionate about my girls and the dance. I had expected more of a fight from my audience, but everyone was respectful and receptive to my philosophy of aesthetics. When I opened the floor to debate, virtually no one offered any challenges and by the end of the ninety-minute class, all but one student—the football player—sided with me. Yes, stripping was art. Absolutely and without qualification.

The one holdout was a young fellow, a ball-cap-wearing jock who loved to hear himself speak. I appreciated his spirited rebuttals and called him Jockstrap. He reminded me of my three linebacker brothers back home, and that put me at ease. I invited him to come to the Magic Gardens to see for himself what I was talking about. I was working that afternoon.

Sure as shit he showed up. Bought me a drink. Said, "Alright you win."

Check Your Head, Part Two

Stripping is a Job

Stripping is a job. It's boring, depressing, fun, funny; the boss sucks, the bitch in the next cubicle is a bitch. The fact that you routinely make three hundred dollars in five hours with no paper trail can make you feel pretty rich, make you ride high on the horse. But when rent time comes and the customers are off somewhere getting their rent together, what's a gal to do? Three out of four weeks a month you can buy twenty-dollar lipsticks and fifty-dollar face creams and eightballs of coke, but when you've got eight hundred dollars' worth of bills and no checks coming and twenty bucks under your mattress, you're fucked. Many girls who quit and get a "real job" say that they work more but have lots more free time; they earn less but seem to have more money.

It took me three years before I realized that to pay my bills, working three or four shifts a week, I needed to stash away eighty bucks a shift. And I learned I was much happier if I put twenty into a special VIVA fund. Pay yourself first! Twenty bucks is one night out, Sunday brunch, a CD. Twenty bucks a shift over two years is six weeks in Morocco, Spain, and Paris. If my car needed work, a car fund was created. This put the money seemingly falling from heaven into perspective. Stripping was a job. I had to use this money that felt—sure—a little like blood money to pay for motherfucking Williams, tampons, and new brakes. It took me another couple years to figure out that I didn't have money enough to sit in coffee shops all day, buy new clothes on a whim, get facials, eat out always. But I had so much cash on hand and so much time to spend it. This is why strippers routinely get out of the business—after ten years of earning fifty thousand to five hundred thousand a year—with nothing to show for it. Why? Because:

Stripping is a Lifestyle

You work 'til three in the morning, wake up at noon sore and hungover with a pile of cash. You're too exhausted to do anything creative or productive. You gotta work later, at nine. So, how to spend the daylight hours? Smoke pot and watch movies. Talk on the phone. Walk around. Buy something. Go out for dinner. Drink.

To do something creative or productive, it's helpful to have a routine. However it's really hard to create a routine with stripping. Even working three nights a week you're completely thrown off the other four. Maybe you can write a short story, maybe show up for band practice. Anything beyond that is damn near impossible.

Time kept on slipping into the future. I'd been dancing almost a year. My college loans went into repayment, I hadn't played my guitar in months, and I was broke. My takeover wasn't exactly going according to plan. Terri would only give me—or anyone—two shifts a week, one shitty, one okay. I'd been going to band auditions but nothing had clicked. I was involved with a boy who took pretty darn good care of me—Johnny Angel—and we were talking about moving in together.

I realized it was probably time to quit town to break my new habits—stripping, late nights, liquor, love—before they broke me.

I'd said I'd only strip for a year (everyone says this), just long enough to pay off my debts. But a year later, I'd barely made a payment. I didn't have any money to move. And if I did move, what would I do for a job? I was still dead-set on having a rock 'n' roll band, scribbling in coffee shops, and taking photographs on the side. Regular nine-to-fives, from what I understood, pretty much precluded any kind of real creative expression. They simply took too much time. Maybe I could strip for one more year, maybe get hired at a couple different clubs, strip five days a week, really haul in the cash...

It was another case of the shoulds. I *should* be doing a lot more. I was wasting my potential, my money, my youth.

Sunday phone calls with the parents didn't help. Why didn't I take the Foreign Service exam? I spoke five languages, three of them fluently. Why not try investment banking? I'd gone to Williams College and was awesome at math. Or I could just move to LA! Everyone raved about my acting abilities, and Mom and Dad knew Mary Hart from *Entertainment Tonight,* which, in the opinion of my pops, was the equivalent of the keys to the kingdom.

In July Katie came to visit me for a week. She and I had met in Tanzania while studying wildlife ecology, conservation, and Swahili. Now she was studying for a PhD in philosophy at the University of Oregon in Eugene.

Katie took one look at my life and was smitten: the feather boas, the wigs and glitter, the subversiveness and the girl-power, the true-grit Bukowski world of stripping. It all stood in sharp contrast to her academic milieu. The Bukowski world had flesh and blood, looked fresh and beautiful compared to the stale head-trips of her philosophy clique.

"Viva, I want your life. Do you think next summer I could work at the Magic? I would sooo love to. I think I could be a stripper."

The idea of Katie as a stripper made me grin. In Africa she was a radical lesbian, well-versed in transgender politics and mired in a codependent S/M relationship with a girlfriend she'd left behind in Iowa. She had a boy's body and short messy brown hair.

"You would totally be a hot stripper. If I can do it, anyone can."

In college I never would have been chosen "Person Most Likely to Become a Stripper." I was a shy tomboy and felt completely isolated and misunderstood amongst the sheltered rich kids. Philosophically it wasn't much of a leap to stripping, but physically it certainly was.

When I thought about what my other college gal pals were doing, the shoulds abated somewhat. Nature-loving Alexa was working for the Department of Natural Resources in Rhode Island. Her job description included raiding goose nests and destroying the eggs to prevent overpopulation. It broke her heart. Sweet Jane was wrapped in a bland brown business suit in Boston, filing papers and wasting her brilliant brain as a subordinate at a nonprofit. Hilary was in med school in Houston and would be for the next decade.

The college set thought what I was doing was ballsy and avant-garde. Occasionally I'd write an epic ten-page letter festooned with press clipping and fliers and send it around the country. They knew I felt inspired and they were proud. One of my anthropology professors even sent a congratulatory postcard when he read my *Willamette Week* debate.

I had to keep my eyes on the prize. There was a lot of work to be done in stripping. I was already part of a creative, vibrant community doing important service-oriented work. Indeed, I was one of the lucky few liberal arts graduates able to brag that I was actually working in my field. Not only that, but stripping was my ultimate childhood dream job: after ten years of diligently studying dance, I had scored one of the highest-paying jobs available to dancers.

I decided to sign on for one more year. I scheduled auditions at a couple other strip clubs. I could move next summer. I could go straight then.

Suddenly it occurred to me that this stripping thing might not be so benign. Maybe it was life-altering, booby-trapped, and ultimately dangerous. Maybe I wouldn't ever be able to get out but would always promise myself "just one more year." Maybe I'd be one of those fifty-year-old strippers working the shag-carpet stages out on East 82nd Avenue. Maybe I loved my job a little too much.

Mary's Club

Portland's got thousands of bars, and well over fifty strip bars. Luck-ily for out-of-town lushes there's *Barfly*, an exhaustive guide to every *boîte* that serves booze. According to *Barfly*, Magic Gardens is known for its "smart, cinematically beautiful strippers who dance to a great soundtrack." But this wasn't always the case; I've encountered a hand-ful of the old guard and they are most emphatically not cinematically beautiful. But they are smart.

Third Avenue in Old Town was known as Suicide Alley until the mid-eighties. You just didn't go there. Not many made the walk north to 4th where the Magic is, either.

One Magic survivor from the seventies came in sporadically with—usually—the same john. She was a ringer for Aileen Wuornos in both looks and gesture: long, sandy blonde hair, an easy dirty smile, mean eyes, and a body that, though petite, said don't-fuckin'-fuck-with-me-I've-been-fuckin'-fucked-enough. She loved me, hated men. "I wouldn't date a man unless you paid me!" she'd cackle, smacking the john in the stomach and then snuggling up to him all romantic-like.

One hot day she was wearing a loose-fitting faded black tank top. On her upper right arm was a tattoo of a butterfly, blue, green, and black, about three inches wide, two inches tall. It was neatly bisected by a four-inch long, one-inch wide scar.

"How'd ya get that scar?" I mewed from the stage, half-naked.

"Knife fight. Some crazy jealous stripper bitch stabbed me in the arm right here in the basement. Thought I was taking her customer." More cackling.

I begged her to let me photograph it, to let me interview her. Could I have her phone number? Any kind of contact info?

"I'm around, sweetheart. I'll run into ya again."

By the time I took the stage, the Magic was a classy joint, de-spite appearances to the contrary, and physical violence was frowned upon. Still, if a girl got touched, she was permitted to wollop the perpetrator.

Our chief competition was Mary's Club, five blocks away on Broad-way and Burnside. Mary's—"Rose City's First Topless"—was

Miss Mona's
Lingerie Show

FEB 7th
9PM

An intimate evening
of show-and-tell
with beautiful women
in their underwear

MARY'S CLUB   129 SW BROADWAY   227-3023

another dive, also featuring classy non-stereotypical dancers and a fine jukebox.

How does a strip club come to have intelligent, beautiful, "non-stereotypical" dancers? Ultimately it boils down to money. If the money is good, good dancers will follow. If working conditions are good, they will stay. In the case of Mary's Club, the average tenure was about fifteen years.

I would have preferred never to have ventured outside the Magic, but with Terri managing, my position was too tenuous, so I struck out to find new stages. I auditioned at Union Jacks first, a glitzy club in the midst of East Burnside's wasteland of used needles and five-dollar whores. Jacks looked like the real-deal strip club: high ceilings, wall-to-wall mirrors, disco balls, and red lights. They had a nice big stage with a pole and a smaller stage by the bar. Four to ten girls worked any given shift. I loathed working with more than two girls; the shifts were longer and the money was unpredictable which spawned competition and hustling. Worse, with an hour to kill between sets, dancers tended to overindulge in liquor and gossip. But I biked across Burnside anyway, toting my duffel bag. Terri made me nervous; I needed a back-up gig.

After checking in with the bar and slamming a shot of tequila, I made my way downstairs to Jacks' enormous, well-appointed dressing room, complete with tanning bed and shower. I pulled on my skintight sequined disco ball dress and black knee-high boots, then promptly took it off ten minutes later to Blondie and Iggy Pop. After my set, the lady bartender informed me that the owner wasn't around and that I'd have to come back and audition for him. Fuck that.

I jumped back on my bike and rode across the Burnside Bridge to Mary's Club. I punched more Iggy Pop and Blondie into the jukebox, peeled off my skintight disco ball dress, and got the job.

Mary's was Portland's oldest strip club. It was named for the owner's wife, Mary, in the fifties. When the marriage ended, the bar was sold to Roy Keller. Roy kept the name and turned it into a piano bar. Between piano sets, Roy hired dancing girls to keep the longshoremen drinking. Soon there was a line around the block for the intermission shows and the piano player was sent packing. Slowly but surely the showgirls showed more and more. Mary's went topless in 1965.

By the time I took the stage, it had been an all-nude revue for a long time—long enough for several of the letters advertising this to have fallen off the dingy marquee.

Keller's daughter Vicki managed Mary's. Her daughters tended bar, cocktailed, and stripped. It was the definition of a mom and pop business.

Mary's was the sleazy, beautifully fucked-up heart of Portland, geographically and metaphorically. Located at downtown's prime intersection where Broadway met Burnside, Mary's iconic neon sign welcomed comers to a city that was still very much a port town, with sailors and shanghai tunnels, ladies of leisure and a thriving criminal element. Walking in off the street, you'd inevitably run into a pimp doing something nefarious or a teenager trying to see a flash of tit. Once inside the bar, your eyes took a full minute to adjust to its cozy red womblike darkness. Around the perimeter were gorgeous murals of stevedores and madames, Mt. Hood looming over them, majestic in the moonlight. To the right was the bar, to the left a pinball machine. In the back was a pool table and a tiny storage space with a microwave and a toaster oven to warm the legally-required menu of frozen pizzas and microwave popcorn.

Although Mary's was the size of the Magic, the layout was so different that it fostered a totally different stripper-customer relationship. The stage was tiny—6' × 8' stage—and was a vertigo-inducing four feet off the floor. Customers who sat at the stage seats had to tilt their heads back to see anything other than platform heels dancing by. Ultimately this meant that the interaction between a dancer and her audience was less intimate and more of a show. The witty repartee and intellectual conversations that were an integral part of my Magic routine wouldn't work from Mary's stage, so I soon authored an arsenal of stage quips, delivered as always in my Marilyn Monroe coo. Like it or not, I had to become a different dancer when I worked at Mary's; the audience was generally too zombified by their hard or fast lives to commune with me from the stage. At Mary's, I was more of a caricature: less heart and soul, more bitchy *bons mots*. However I had to admit it was a relief from the blood-sweat-&-tears rock star stuff going down at the Magic. Mary's was my job; Magic was my passion.

Still, both places took hold of my heart equally, and I fell in love with the more down-to-earth Mary's girls as often and as hard as I did with Magic's psychotic beautiful dreamers.

I ❤ My Volvo

Shortly after I started dancing at Mary's, around the time Johnny Angel and I moved in together, Hundred Dollar Dave began to visit the Magic more frequently. He'd probably been temporarily eighty-sixed from Sassy's, his usual hangout, and was in need of a new place to play his sub-legal mind games. The Magic day shift was a perfect playground.

The first time I made really big money off of Dave—four hundred and fifty bucks in one shift—I felt like I'd magically morphed into an Upper Eastside debutante. All I'd done was wear my panties backwards, spank a girl's bottom, and get spanked some myself and suddenly I was RICH! It was the first windfall of my life.

I biked home to Johnny Angel ecstatic.

"Dress up. I'm taking you out to dinner."

It was a hot August afternoon. I put on a classy cream-colored A-line dress (I did relish the Jackie O yuppie-wife role on occasion). Angel changed his Angry Samoans t-shirt and jeans for a sea-green guayabera and nice slacks. We walked down Burnside and up Park Avenue, arm in arm, to the Brasserie Montmarte, the chicest place I could imagine. We enjoyed ice-cold vodka martinis at the Brasserie's beautiful mahogany bar, then moved to a romantic table overlooking a jazz trio. I splurged on a bottle of white wine, escargots, and soups-salads-entrees for both of us. The bill came to ninety bucks. Absolute decadence. Stripping was a dream job.

Hundred Dollar Dave started coming in regularly. My next windfall I spent on fancy designer sunglasses. After a couple more visits, I had enough cash squirreled away in my desk drawer to buy a 1982 white Volvo station wagon for $1400.

That did it. I was officially solvent, officially an adult, and master of my own destiny. More importantly, my dad finally seemed to think so, too.

Growing up the eldest of four kids in a family with no disposable income, a car of my own was never in the cards. But I had always wanted one, always wanted a Volvo. My dad owned Volvos since I was brought home from the hospital in a dark green 1972 sedan. Still Daddy's little girl, I would settle for nothing less. By age fourteen Volvos had become an absolute fetish for me: I loved how solid, how European, how delightfully boxy and colorful they were; I loved the way the Volvo engine sounded when it turned over, loved the crunch of the doors as they closed. Plus you could fit an entire drum set, bass cabinet, guitar amp, and three guitars in the back of a Volvo wagon.

When I finally had a car—a VOLVO—of my own, it became neutral territory in my weekly conversations with my parents. Neither pa nor ma really wanted to hear anything about Mona's fabulous cabarets, Teresa's revolutionary public health crusade, or my invitations to lecture at local colleges on stripping as art. That meant there was precious little to talk about, unless I happened to be shooting an independent film or felt like indulging them with talk about graduate school or taking the Foreign Service exam. Once I got a Volvo, though, and with my stripping money, the job seemed to elicit a bit of respect, at least from my dad.

"Have you checked your oil?"

"You might want to get it waxed before winter."

"Make sure the air conditioning fluid is at the right level, otherwise your power steering could go out."

Mom hung up during car talk. She preferred to hear about Johnny Angel and what wonderful care he was taking of me, at which point Dad would hang up.

My poor parents. Sometimes it was all I could do not to scream, "At least I'm HAPPY! At least I'm ALIVE! At least I'm OFF ANTI-DEPRESSANTS and paying my rent, my college loans, my bills!" But ultimately you can never make anyone happy, least of all your parents.

Still it doesn't really do to stop trying. One day I'll have a Volvo and a day job and maybe even a baby and those Sunday phone calls will be easy as pie.

The Shoulds

As hard as it is to please your parents, it is infinitely harder to please yourself.

It was late summer. Mona was hosting a barbeque at the quaint cottage on Liebe Street she shared with her boyfriend Lucian. I'd spent the day nursing a hangover: greasy breakfast at one in the afternoon, a blow job for Johnny Angel in Sin City's porn arcade, a short pink skirt and a white cotton halter. My hangover felt like a reward and I was going to enjoy it.

The night before I'd debuted at the Satyricon as the keyboardist for my friends' band Spectator Pump. Earlier in the evening I'd performed an ornate burlesque performance at the Mark Woolley Gallery. The fancy art space had commissioned a Viva Las Vegas striptease to celebrate the opening of their new show, "Birds." I wore a feather wig festooned with fake birds from the craft store and sported fake flowers on my naughty parts. During the striptease (to a Mozart aria), I plucked off each flower and handed it to a member of the well-heeled audience. The big orchid decorating my snatch I'd serendipitously bequeathed to the president of the Audubon Society. Coincidences like this remind me there is a God.

Angel had outdone himself, chauffeuring me around downtown with not one but two costume changes plus instruments packed into the Volvo. He'd even kept his drinking in check, and performed the art gallery how-d'ya-dos like the sincere Amherst grad he was deep down under his Irish sneer.

Mo's barbeque was rocking by the time we arrived. Twenty people milled around the garden, and a kiddie pool harbored a handful of kids. Rain greeted us as we walked up the path to the house. She was already wasted.

"Viva! Oh I love you, Viva! Viva, I want you to meet my date. His name is… uh…"

Names were obviously unimportant. The guy was tan and tattooed and well-built, the usual blue-collar boy-toy Rain cottoned to since her recent split from Christian, her longtime lover. Since the breakup she'd been on more of a bender than usual.

I shook the guy's hand. "Viva. Pleased to meet you."

"This is Viva. I love her." Rain was slurring badly, but her giggle was intact. "Hi, Johnny!"

Angel grunted. He was unimpressed with my stripper friends and jealous of my time.

I walked into the house. On the right was a huge closet bursting with vintage coats (Mona had converted most of the house into her own personal walk-in closet). On the left was the bathroom, painted black and filled with candles. Mona spent most of her time in there, in the bath, with a bong. She no longer worked. Lucian took care of everything and babied her in every way. And she despised him for it.

"Hey, Mo! The place looks great!"

Mo was at the dining room table with Pink and Teresa and four people I didn't recognize.

"V! Come here and have a little smoke. There's sangria in the kitchen and beer and champagne. And a bottle of whiskey kicking around somewhere…"

I walked into the kitchen where Lucian was whipping up a four-course feast. There was gumbo on the back burner and a large platter of roasted veggies fresh off the grill. Lucian was in the middle of basting garlic bread. He washed the garlic off his hands and poured me a glass of sangria.

"How's it going, Lucian? Smells delicious."

"She's off her rocker. She was screaming and crying all morning. My nerves are shot."

"You deserve a medal, hon, or at least some more of this." I indicated the sangria. "Poor Lucian, the luckiest guy in town. I know she's been a mess lately. We need to get her working on another cabaret."

"I know and I try and encourage her, but she says she's too depressed. I don't know what to do, Viva."

"I'll take her out for tea this week. Like I said, you deserve a medal. We all appreciate your taking care of her. I mean, somebody's got to."

I kissed Lucian on the cheek, grabbed two beers, plucked Johnny off the couch, and steered him outside. It was evident that he wasn't going to last long. We'd only been at the party for five minutes and already he was grumbling. He wasn't happy unless he had my undivided attention.

Out in the yard Lawyer Patty was talking to Mia about law school. English Dave and Fat Jerry and Mick the cabbie passed a pipe around the picnic table, which was heaped with salads, condiments, and Japanese sweets. The sun was just beginning to dip behind the West Hills and Portland looked like the Garden of Eden: a deep pink valley covered with magnificent evergreens, skyscrapers sparkling in the twilight, and bridges gleaming in sharp relief in the distance, mustard yellow, brick red, and bright white.

I turned my back to the party and sighed. I loved these people—LOVED THEM—but I couldn't live like them, spending days in the bath, watching daytime TV and playing video games, stoned out of my gourd, then hitting the town when darkness finally fell and staying out 'til 3 AM every night, dressed up and messed up. It was becoming sadly apparent that stripping would never be enough for me. Johnny Angel would never be enough. Even the rock 'n' roll wasn't going to be enough.

What was it the Gospel of Thomas said? If you don't bring forth what is inside you, that which is inside you will kill you. If you do bring forth what is inside you, that which is inside you will be your salvation. Well, clearly I was doomed. I felt like I had too much inside me to bring forth. The weight of it was suffocating me.

I had an enduring superhero complex. Perhaps every smarty-pants overachieving girl does; it goes along with the anorexia, the Virginia Woolf, the slashed wrists. I had great and noble longings: to help humanity, to sacrifice any and all personal pleasures for the greater good—Save the Whales, Save Central Africa, Save Rock 'n' Roll—and thereby win my own salvation. But the great and noble longings were insatiable and were consuming me from the inside out. The goddamn motherfucking SHOULDS.

I left the party with my beer to walk around the block and sort out my sudden dissatisfaction. I knew I had to formulate an escape plan or I'd be caught in the same trap as Mona, brilliant but drowning in a cozy codependency, her wasted talent poisoning her from within.

The keynote speaker at my high school graduation had admonished us all to follow our bliss, to pursue that which made us joyful that we might be joyful and share that joy. But my goddamn bliss was all over the map. Stripping brought me much joy, but I had to admit it was a dead end. So what next? I loved living abroad and learning languages. Maybe I could do the Graham Greene thing, join the Foreign Service and write inspired musings from abroad. But then what about rock 'n' roll? You can't travel very well with electric guitars and vintage amplifiers. And rock 'n' roll was an American conceit. I didn't see it going over quite the same way in Bali or Zanzibar. As a rock 'n' roller I was beholden to my cultural milieu. Alright, fuck the Foreign Service. What about grad school? But in what? Writing? Maybe photography? I loved photography… But an MFA was expensive and impractical. What about medicine? I'd always been fascinated by Chinese medicine and naturopathy, and the parents would be thrilled. But wasn't I an artist? I would wilt and die working in a hospital or doctor's office.

The only thing that kept the shoulds at bay was my time on stage. Stripping was so liberating in that it let my frantic mind focus in the glare of the red lights. Stripping was my saviour. Still I knew better than to get too comfortable. I was twenty-three for fuck's sake.

I returned to the party and found Johnny scowling where I'd left him. He looked super hot, like JFK Jr. but skinnier, more skateboarder, and with that punk rock know-it-all cynicism I found so attractive.

"Let's get out of here," I said.

Angel smiled for the first time all evening.

"Okay," he said shyly, glad for the attention. He loved me alright. I kissed him mercenarily. Angel was a great support system; he'd do anything for me. But ultimately I felt that he, too, wanted me in a cage. Still I'd have to end up in a cage sooner or later. That's life, right?

Maybe I could keep stripping long enough to figure out what sort of cages were out there. I had so many talents, so many rich experiences—certainly I could find some job that wouldn't be dehumanizing, some place I could sell my soul for at least slightly more than the going rate. Didn't I deserve that? With my lofty ideals and intention to save all of humanity by shining sterling example?

Johnny was driving. I hadn't spoken a word since Mona's and now we were almost home. The malaise was enveloping me, a persistent notion that there must be more to life than I'd ferreted out. We pulled into the driveway of our cozy new duplex.

"Well, that was fun," Angel quipped sarcastically.

"Fuck you," I snarled, slamming the car door. I would blame this sudden depression on him, although he had nothing to do with it. That's what ya get when you date an overindulged overachiever. By the time he opened the front door I was in tears. *There must be more! There must be more!*

"What's wrong, baby?"

"Fuck you! Leave me alone!"

I stomped up to the bedroom and cried myself to sleep. I didn't need a new job; I needed a lobotomy.

Big Al Et Al

Poor Viva. Grandma and Pops always told me that my love of rock 'n' roll was tempting eternal damnation. But how could I refuse it? It was my one enduring love from the moment I heard the *Grease* soundtrack (which I promptly stole from my elementary school library).

I moved to Portland with every intention of devoting myself to rock 'n' roll. And while it's true Mona and her cabarets were mighty distracting, I could only blame myself when, after a year and a half, I hadn't written a single song and my Stratocaster was covered with dust. I had tried to find a band, going on lots of auditions and eventually landing the gig in Spectator Pump, but I loathed playing keyboards. Chrissie Hynde didn't play keyboards. Chrissie Hynde played guitar.

Down at the office, the Magic Gardens regulars had become accustomed to my constant lament that I didn't have a band. One of them finally did something about it. Big Al.

Why do men go to strip clubs, anyway? This is a matter of enduring and contentious debate. Most folks unfamiliar with the industry assume men come in to get off—that the interaction is purely sexual and devoid of intimacy, and therefore pathetic and mercenary. Of course I think it's quite the opposite. I prefer to think that my boys come to the strip bar for conviviality, for something more human and more lovely than the usual TV in the corner. And really, which is more intimate: a sports bar or a tit bar? Which is healthier for your heart, your conscience? Should you be exposed to a wall of brain-melting telemundo or a smiling stripper effervescing naked onstage?

Over time a gal acquires "regulars"—customers who show up at every shift and who can be counted on to pay her rent/mortgage/car payment. What a regular gets in return is special access to his/her gal's thoughts and emotions—something frequently called, in lay terms, "friendship."

A regular becomes a regular for many reasons. Perhaps he loves the inimitable way his gal dances. Maybe he has a rich fantasy life in which she plays the starring role. Maybe he loves the music she plays. Or maybe they both have a deep love of Russian literature. A successful stripper learns quickly how to be all things to all people—a philosopher, psychologist, politician, and pinup model—all in the course of a fifteen-minute set.

My two all-time favorite regulars were Van and Al. Van was a former musician, Al an amateur art critic. Both got under my skin by inquiring repeatedly after my still-nascent music career. In the end, Van bought me a Camaro-red Gibson SG, but it was Big Al's stubborn insistence that got me to actually plug the thing into my Sears Silvertone amplifier and take the stage at Satyricon.

Big Al was a thirty-something high-tech worker who knew the punk rock lexicon word for word. I'd seen him around—he was finger-bangin'-Rose's regular and was also a huge fan of Mona and regularly sent her epic critiques of her cabarets. When Al heard that I hoped to start a band, he took it as his personal mission to see that I did. He'd buy table dances and, while I was dancing naked a foot from his face, badger me. Why wasn't I playing music? He gave me Germs CDs and Sex Pistols posters and transcriptions of Clash lyrics. Eventually he concocted a scheme.

Al had written a screenplay about the late great pornstar John Holmes with Holmes' widow in Reno, Nevada. Over a table dance, he told me that he needed a soundtrack. He later brought in the screenplay with a note that I had four weeks to come up with a theme song for it. Then he came in every week for more table dances to mark my progress.

Al's plan worked. In two months I created a precious pop song called "Red Hot," complete with sampled kitten/sex noises mixed under raw guitar tracks and keyboard licks.

I was terrified handing over the tape. Singing and playing music was as nude as I got. Big Al actually got tears in his eyes as he caressed the cassette. He took it home and, two weeks later, returned with a two-page review and a bottle of booze to congratulate me. Six months later I would have my own band, The Licks, whose hit song was "Red Hot."

TO: *Viva "If I Hear One More EVERCLEAR Song, I Swear I'll Start Slashing My Wrists With A Guitar Pick" Las Vegas, Amp Queen, Guitar Goddess*
RE: *RED HOT*

Dear Viva:
Many thanks for making this tape for me! As you know, my forte is writing theater reviews for Miss Mona's excesses. I am not a rock critic, but since you're anxiously awaiting some feedback on your work, I'll give it my best shot:
The song, RED HOT, begins with the disembodied, electronic mewing of kitties, then breaks in with your breathless singing, while still more sterile, robotic mewing goes on in the background. "Meow, meow, meow," it's like listening to Yoko Ono reincarnated as a cat. The guitar work is very reminiscent of the WHO's Pete Townsend; lots of steady power-chords that do not require the use of the pinkie finger. This song is going to work out great with my video, because I asked Nikki to hold up that fat, sumo wrestler cat

of hers for the camera. I am very happy with the tape, and I will do my best to put something together you can be proud of—something you can show your grandkids!

On the last day Mia worked at the Magic Gardens, I asked her why, after everything she'd been through, would she ever go back to working at Starbucks for 50¢ over minimum wage. I mean, she had thousands stacked up from dancing and working at Frolic's, why would she go back to dragging herself out of bed at four in the morning to serve coffee to a bunch of smiling, vapid yuppie idiots? Although I already knew why, it still meant a lot to me that she gave me an honest answer; she said, "To be around normal people again, even for 20 hours a week." But you, you don't like to be around normal people. Like Mona, you have been cursed with this creative streak that will not allow you the simple luxury of being satisfied. I'll never forget the time we were sitting at the bar at Mary's (it was the night of that stupid competition I came up with), and this black guy comes in the door and you stopped him and ran your finger along the scar on his face and asked him if he was all right. You probably don't even remember this, but I'll never forget it. This guy was in some pretty bad shape, and he didn't look like he had a nickel, and when you ran your finger along the left side of his face I remember thinking how few people on this planet would ever extend that type of human kindness to a person that was that far out from their social clique. It actually reminded me of The Story of Job, in the Bible; it was really that profound.

You are a beautiful person in a rough business. I really wonder how you survive it intact. As I'm sure you know, there are a lot of "lost souls" here in this soggy, rain-soaked town of Portland, Oregon—more so, perhaps, than anywhere else. There are lots of people just "hiding out" here (Rose was telling me that the guitarist for Supertramp hangs out there at Tommy's Too). I think we're both living here at the right time—my book, your band, this is going to be a great year!

Love, Alan O.

P.S. How's this for a band name? VIVA LAS VEGAS AND HER ALCOHOLIC SKATEBOARDERS

P.P.S. Billy Idol wore sweatbands on stage, I think it's the next big thing!

How to Strip, Part Three

Pink Marilyn sequined
    baby doll dress
Pink G-string
Black velvet dress
Black panties
Black bra
Black bowtie
Disco ball dress
Leopard tie-front half-shirt
Leopard thong
"How Swede It Is" t-shirt
Cars Candy-O t-shirt
White skirt
White shorts

White cotton bra & panty set
Blue wool half-sweater
Orange tie-front half-shirt
Groovy flowered thong
Blue silk robe w/dragon
    embroidery
Make-up bag, incl. Almay
    mascara and eyeliner,
    Revlon ColorStay lip-
    stick in Vixen and Shell,
    Mac powder, arnica gel,
    glitter eye gel, guitar
    picks, $60
Red North Face backpack

Teresa and I had just finished lunch at the Thai Peacock after working the day shift together at Mary's. I was trying to kill a couple hours until Johnny's bartending shift ended at six thirty. I meandered down Oak Street, admiring the fall colors. Johnny and I were heading to Seattle in the morning, and I was thrilled to be getting out of town for a couple days. As I approached Paranoid Park, my heart sank. The sidewalk alongside my precious Volvo was glittering with shattered glass. The fucking street punks had broken the window.

I looked inside the car, afraid of what I'd find. Of course they'd taken my stripper bag: a nice North Face mountaineering backpack that was bulging with outfits. Why had I left it in the car anyway? And right next to Paranoid Park? Why hadn't I just brought it to lunch with me? Thank God my shoe suitcase was still in the car; my shoes were irreplaceable, and the most expensive part of my wardrobe. Nobody wanted a shitty old vintage suitcase, even if it did contain one-of-a-kind seven-inch leopard-print wooden platforms, seven-inch blue glitter Lucite stilettos, and knee-high black leather fuck-me boots that I bought on a trip to New York City. Fucking punks. What were they going to do with a bunch of G-strings and half-shirts? Still, losing the outfits was mostly an inconvenience. I was far more upset that the assholes had violated my car. I brushed the glass off the seat and drove to the Magic, where Johnny had been picking up shifts as a day bartender.

"VIVA!!!"

I always received a hero's welcome when I walked into the Magic, not to mention several free drinks. But I wasn't in the mood today.

"Johnny, can you come talk to me for a second? Outside?"

The regulars looked uncomfortably from me to him. He wiped his hands on a bar towel and followed me to the foyer.

"Fucking street kids broke into my car and took my stripper bag!" I was almost in tears, thinking how my carelessness had cost me. Would our trip to Seattle be spoiled now, too? I looked forward to our Seattle trips more than anything. It was so rare that Johnny and I got the same two consecutive days off that it was bound to be a year before it would happen again.

"I'm so sorry, babe. Do you want me to call the cops?"

"I don't know. I guess so. What are they gonna do? I highly doubt a backpack filled with panties will be high on their list of priorities."

"Was there cash in there?"

"Yeah, but only sixty bucks. I had a miserable shift, even though it was fun to work with Teresa."

"Come inside, have a drink, and wait for the fuzz."

"No. I don't want to talk to anyone. I'm too pissed off. I'll wait for them by the car. Tell them to meet me on Davis."

I sat outside on the curb, practicing deep breathing until the cops showed up. I filed a police report, then headed home, miserable. My next shift was the night we were getting back from Seattle. How was I going to replace my wardrobe by then?

The next morning Johnny and I got coffee and croissants and ate them at an auto glass shop while my window was replaced. We were on the road by noon, and shopping four hours later.

Like most strippers I knew, I spent plenty on shoes and music. That was, after all, all you had on at the end of the day. However, when it came to outfits I was very frugal. Mostly I shopped at discount places like Nordstrom Rack and Ross Dress for Less, where matching bra-and-panty sets ran about ten bucks, and cute sundresses and half sweaters could be found in the Junior's department. The Rave at the mall was perfect for the sluttier stuff all the high school girls were wearing: super-short shorts and skirts, cheap velvet dresses, and anything you could possibly want in leopard print. Occasionally I would splurge at Frederick's of Hollywood or Spartacus Leathers if they had something I simply had to have, like a rubber thong, elegant corset, or purrfect baby-doll slip.

Seattle had many of the same chain stores as Portland, but I didn't exactly know where they were. Luckily Johnny was more than game to stripper shop. He grinned like a schoolboy as he sat on various couches, enjoying the fashion show as I reinvented my wardrobe. I found a new black velvet dress at the Metro in the University District. Thank God! I couldn't do my classy act without a black velvet dress. I also found a fishnet-and-fringe skirt on sale for eight dollars and a tight silver camisole for seven. I was thrilled to find a new fuzzy sweater—in pink angora!—and a wool Catholic schoolgirl skirt at Buffalo Exchange. Finally, at Red Light, I found my new security blanket: a vintage black silk robe embroidered with flowers. A robe was *de rigueur* for my act: I covered up immediately after each striptease, demurely hiding my nudity only seconds after flaunting it, magically morphing back into a shy Midwesterner as I stepped down from the stage to mix with my audience.

By five thirty, Angel and I were headed downtown to Nordstrom Rack on Pike Street, where I found a half-dozen thongs and G-strings for two bucks a piece, and an adorable pink-and-white striped bra-and-panty set that had little hearts and I Love Yous on them. This latter was absolutely imperative for my short-white-skirt act. Now I just needed a short white skirt. I'd have to hit the Rave in Portland before my shift. There was no way I could work without a short white skirt. And I'd try to hit Spartacus, too, to get some new PVC vixen wear to match my fuck-me boots.

As a reward for Angel's infinite patience, I let him look at records for a full half-hour before we went to a fancy dinner at the Flying Fish. There I toasted him with a martini.

"Angel Baby, thanks for goin' to all the girly stores with me today. I'm so relieved to have new duds. I hope all this shopping isn't ruining the trip for you."

"Are you kidding me? So far this is the best Seattle trip ever."

I blew the sweet boy a kiss and promised him further rewards when we got back to our hotel room.

Exotic

As luck would have it, my fairy godmother was waiting in the wings that winter with a new assignment that would keep the shoulds at bay for a little while longer, an assignment that augmented the Viva Las Vegas show by committing my obstreperous coffee shop musings to the sanctity of printed matter. Frank Fallaice, the publisher of West Coast skin rag *Exotic Magazine,* asked me to come on board as music editor.

Frank had kept tabs on me ever since my appearance in the *Willamette Week.* He'd seen that I could write and had noticed my various musical endeavors. One afternoon we met for coffee at Umbra Penumbra where he offered me the job.

I was skeptical. I wasn't a fan of the industry magazines, filled with tacky ads for escorts and even tackier writing about the goings-on at the clubs and how much the vapid chick on the cover loved (a) dolphins, (b) guns, or (c) motorcycles. I preferred *Danzine's* by-strippers for-strippers style.

Wait a minute… If I were editor, I could do exactly as I pleased, right? I could do the by-strippers, for-strippers stuff in the middle of the escort ads!

I told Frank I'd think about it. It was a wonderful opportunity, and I had a policy of saying yes to fate, whatever it presented. Plus it must be said that Frank's *Exotic* was different from the run-of-the-mill industry garbage. His aesthetic was more intelligent, more hip, more rock-n-roll. He ran articles about Lenny Bruce and Bunny Yeager. He gave covers to promising young local photographers. He put art and speech ahead of advertising and politics. Honestly, he was brilliant. And cute.

The Gospel

according to Viva Las Vegas ♥ "the laziest gal downtown"

What would it mean for Viva to climb astride *Exotic?* Would it ruin my street-cred? Would I be selling out? What would *Danzine* do?

Danzine served its niche market well, but *Exotic* offered far better distribution. As editor I could bring a little *Danzine* to the stereotype-laden *Exotic* world. Why let the big-boobed dolphin-loving girls get all the copy?

Oftentimes throughout my stripping career, I've been reminded of the Sunday School song, "This little light of mine, I'm gonna let it shine." Stripping let me do that with no—ahem—strings attached. Frank's *Exotic Magazine* promised me the same package. I took the gig.

Portland permits paradoxes to exist. It's just easy enough to survive that a person can conceivably plant each foot firmly in opposite spheres. This is great for artists and musicians, as long as they have no pesky visions of grandeur (i.e., an itty bit of "success"). You'll never meet so many down-to-earth rich girls, slumming cops, functioning alcoholics, or brilliant strippers anywhere else. Portland, for better or worse, is a swamp in which anything will grow. I was a stripper and damn proud of it. Now, thanks to *Exotic Magazine,* I would be preaching on the side. In honor of my dad the Reverend, I titled my monthly column "The Gospel According to Viva Las Vegas." In honor of Marlene Dietrich, I subtitled it "The Laziest Gal Downtown," riffing on her song "The Laziest Gal in Town." (I knew I couldn't copy the song title verbatim. Mona was the laziest gal in town, after all. Everyone knew that. But she lived in the 'burbs.)

Within weeks after "The Gospel" premiered, I'd pissed off most of the Mary's girls by insisting in print that chick singers like Natalie Merchant and Alanis Morrisette had no business being played at strip clubs. Later more folks bristled when I wrote about getting wasted with a hugely pregnant stranger at a Mudhoney show while putting out cigarettes on people's arms. I had a pesky notion that if no one was pissed off by my writing, I'd accidentally committed JOURNALISM, the worst sin.

Music criticism was never my favorite genre. Music should be listened to, not written about. Soon I'd careened off the music editor path to pen stuff about boot shines, smoking fetishes, and political pains-in-my-ass. I still wrote about music, interviewing my favorite bands live over beer in their dressing rooms, but "The Gospel" became increasingly philosophical and heartfelt, and it amazed me how many people—customers especially—read it religiously for precisely that content. Every now and then I'd scribble a little fluff piece for the bored strippers to read between sets, but mostly I authored soul-baring stuff that terrified me when I saw it in print. Talk about all-nude! My writing was the real deal, the under-the-skin stuff. And the guys loved it.

Customers always want to get to know you. They want to know about your cats, your hometown, your broken heart. Lord knows why. Perhaps they are even more beguiled into thinking they have an actual connection (i.e., relationship) with you if they know the ins and outs of your day-to-day.

And my day-to-day was absolutely fabulous. Woke up at eight, went for a swim, had a leisurely coffee date with Johnny Angel. Went CD shopping, browsed for hours at Powell's Books, caught a matinee. Had long laughter-filled dinners at Fellini, arguing about the relative merits of the Clash, Bruce Springsteen, and the Pretenders. Let the evening melt into night and caught a rock show at Satyricon. Occasionally I'd strip for five hours. There was enough time to have a rock 'n' roll band, paint my nails, and fight the powers that be. There was enough money for organic groceries, thrift store shopping junkets, and trips out of town. And now I could enjoy it again as my work at *Exotic,* an actual job with an actual office and an actual distribution run of seventy-five thousand, would temporarily assuage the shoulds.

Another Saturday Night

Bang! Bang! Bang!
Three shots rang out, piercing the Saturday night festivities like a dagger in a wedding cake. I jumped up from my hummus plate and headed outside, where the usual cacophony of Fellini's colorful peacocks was suddenly stilled into an echoing silence. Across 6th Avenue

on Davis Street a car peeled away into the night. In the glare of the parking lot lights I could make out a body. I ran across the street and scaled the fence along with several others.

The Hispanic man was mortally wounded, gasping desperately for air as blood soaked his jacket. One of Satyricon's resident rockers cradled the man's head while I held his hand.

"Don't worry, mister. You're gonna be just fine. Help is on the way," I said calmly, then turned to the bystanders and hissed, "Call a fucking ambulance!"

Mona scampered the long way around the lot in her platform heels. Both she and Teresa had been at an art opening and were dressed in full showgirl regalia, with elaborate headdresses and fringed bras and almost nothing below the waist. Mona's superhero was clearly visible through her fishnets, and Teresa's pussy was festooned with a big red flower and nothing more.

"Oh my God. Holy shit. Does anyone have a light?"

"Mona! Shhh!" I shot her a look and she bit her fist.

The wounded man had a look of terror in his eyes. Chances were the guy didn't speak English, but I hoped he could understand at least three words. Thinking that I would like to hear them if I were about to die, I pressed his hand tighter and said, "I love you. I love you. I love you."

The man couldn't take in air. His eyelids fluttered, his eyes rolled back, and he stopped struggling.

"He's gone," said the rocker.

I covered my eyes with my free hand.

"Oh God," whimpered Mona.

Suddenly a platoon of police descended along with an ambulance, but silently, without sirens or lights. A lady cop approached us.

"Clear the area. Nothing to see here. Clear the area immediately."

I tried to speak to her, to tell her about the car that sped away, to file a witness report.

"Just clear the area, ma'am. Now."

Stunned, our little gang crossed back to Fellini, where a crowd had gathered. We watched as paramedics removed the body and the police cordoned off the parking lot.

"Jesus, Viva. Somebody gets shot and you just run right over there? That's not exactly safe. Are you okay?"

The last thing I needed was a scolding from Johnny. "No I'm not okay. That guy just died in front of me, and I bet it won't even appear in the paper." I was deeply moved but preferred to exhibit anger rather than grief. I headed to our usual corner table, where Mona's headdress was buried in Lucian's lap. Teresa arrived with a tray of shots.

"Kamikazes. Jesus Christ. Did anyone know the guy? Did he have a name? No? Well, then. To our departed friend! May he know peace…"

Mona interrupted the toast with a heartbroken wail, but roused herself from Lucian's lap long enough to down two shots. I did a shot and turned to Angel.

"Johnny baby, can I have a cigarette?" I didn't smoke but my nerves were stretched so taut I thought they'd snap. "On second thought, can we just get the fuck out of here?"

Angel threw a twenty on the table and grabbed our coats. My legs felt like leaden weights and my heart like a dead flower. I leaned on Johnny heavily as we walked to the Park Blocks to the car.

"Angel, this town is too dark for me. What the fuck? That guy fucking died. I was holding his hand…"

I didn't want to cry. I was not gonna cry. I went on the offensive.

"You know what, Johnny? I don't think I've seen a sunrise since I moved here."

"Baby, you get up earlier than anyone we know. I've never known anyone to jump out of bed like you, raring to go."

"I know. But I could get up earlier. I want to see the sunrise. I've always loved the dawn. I love to get up when it's still dark and nobody else is awake and the world is mine. I love to live healthfully. I love healthy people. Johnny, we live in fucking bars!"

The sob lodged in my throat wasn't going away.

"I wanna get the fuck out of here. Let's move to Minnesota… I bet you ten bucks no one reports on that murder. That guy has a family somewhere and they won't ever know…"

I choked on my words and collapsed into Johnny's arms, shaking with emotion, howling like a woebegone dog.

"Give me the keys, baby. I'll drive. And I'll move to Minnesota with you in a heartbeat. Just please don't cry. I hate to see you sad."

Back at the house I washed the streaked makeup off my face and climbed into bed. I looked at the clock. 1 AM. What time did the sun rise anyway? Five thirty? Six? Would I ever see it again?

I woke up at eight the next morning and went for a run. I checked the afternoon edition of the *Oregonian* for several days, looking for information on the dead Mexican. Eventually I searched the Internet for "Man shot on bus mall," but to no avail. Just another nobody, sacrificed to the night.

How to Strip, Part Four

Don't Leave Home Without

Ramones
Muddy Frankenstein
Chrome Cranks
The Cramps
The Cars
The Smiths
The Vaselines
Blondie
Buzzcocks
Berlin
John Spencer Blues
    Explosion
Boss Hog
Butter 08
The Clash
Black Crowes
Police

Jonathan Richman + the
    Modern Lovers
Devo
Detroit Cobras
Thee Headcoatees
White Stripes
Rolling Stones (fifteen al-
    bums +)
Kinks
Suicide
Joan Jett and the Blackhearts
Elvis Costello
Prince
J. Geils Band
Country Teasers
The Makers
Tom Waits

MC5
Missing Persons
The Beatles
Mott the Hoople
Generation X
T. Rex
Joe Jackson
Serge Gainsbourg
Black Sabbath
Johnny Cash
Bob Dylan
Getz/Gilberto
Cream
AC/DC
Donovan
The Damned
The Sweet
Velvet Underground
Lou Reed
Flamin' Groovies
Pretenders
Beach Boys
Buddy Holly
Desmond Dekker
Koko Taylor
Michael Jackson

The Who (five albums +)
David Bowie (six albums +)
Screamin' Jay Hawkins
Andre Williams
Ella Fitzgerald
Billie Holiday
Jimi Hendrix
The Doors
Iggy and the Stooges
Dead Boys
New York Dolls
Johnny Thunders and the
    Heartbreakers
Tom Petty and the
    Heartbreakers
Manfred Mann
Tommy James and the
    Shondells
Siouxsie and the Banshees
Gaunt
The Specials
Various punk comps
Various '80s comps
Various '70s comps
Various '60s comps
Christmas comps (seasonal)

Soundtracks: *Repo Man; Lock, Stock and Two Smoking Barrels; Jesus' Son; Trainspotting; Velvet Goldmine; Crooklyn; Jackie Brown; Boogie Nights; Swingers; Girl 6; Pump Up the Volume; The Harder They Come; Grease; Rushmore*

Suck It & See

Many of us were getting hungry for change. Pink was sick of working at jackshacks and had gone back to school, hoping to soon be a research assistant at OHSU. Mona's last two cabarets had been cancelled;
she was still ensconced on the Eastside, smoking pot and playing video
games while Lucian supported her. A Mona sighting was an increasingly rare thing. Perhaps most unusual of all, Rain had stopped drinking. Rain could down a whole bottle of vodka over the course of a day. I
couldn't believe she'd been able to quit. Was she worried about putting
on weight? Her tits were getting huge, but that didn't seem like such
a problem. Teresa was kicking ass. She'd all but retired from dancing
and was working hard at turning *Danzine* into a legitimate nonprofit.
She spent long days at the library researching and applying for grants
and was shopping around for office space. The City of Portland had
contracted with her to do "harm reduction," including needle exchange
and STD awareness on the streets, so she was actually making a bit of
dough. How she supplemented that income was the subject of rumor
and speculation. However she did it, it was clear that with all her sugar
daddies, mommies, grandpas, and uncles she'd never have to pay for a
meal again.

I was plugging away at *Exotic*, interviewing bands and rocking out
with my own. My plate was full, but not so full that I didn't jump
when I was offered a juicy part in a big-budget extended-length music
video that was shooting locally. The directors knew me from the Magic.
Would I / could I play a hooker?

I've been an actress since I popped out of the womb. During my
tumultuous teen years, acting was the only time I felt comfortable in
my own skin. Somehow, even as the innocent, naïve, head-of-the-class
preacher's daughter, I always got cast in the role of the hussy. My first
kiss and French kiss were both onstage. I always seemed to wind up in
a state of undress, too, something completely out of character for me
offstage. I was so body obsessed and self-loathing that I never once
donned a swimsuit between the ages of ten and twenty.

In Portland I'd been cast in several films. Frequently film folks

Suck It & See

A Film by Jacob Pander

PUSSYFOOT
ARTISTS AND TRACKS FEATURED

Fantastic Plastic Machine "Green Door"

Howie B "Only If It Hurts"

Spacer "Jeffrey Poindexter's Maximum Load"

Hyper Crad "3" (Back Door Mix)

Chari Chari "Favourite Final Geisha Show"

Inevidence "Cum Dancing"

DJ Miku "Pink Planet"

would find me at the Magic and ask if I'd ever considered acting. At which point I'd launch into a recitation of my extensive resumé and, soon after, find myself in front of the camera for a low-budget music video/student film/art project. But this film was gonna be different. This time I'd be getting PAID.

Resident Portland artists the Pander Brothers had won an international competition to direct a six-part thirty-minute music video for British hip-hop impresario Howie B. The idea was an homage to seventies soft-core films like *Émmanuelle.*

The Panders were well known in our scene. Lucian had worked with them extensively, so they knew us strippers well, too. When it came time to cast their soft-core short film, they knew exactly who to ask.

Two girls from the Magic were cast in the lead roles—bisexual nymphomaniacs who torment an older gentleman with their hotness. Mona was commissioned to produce a retro burlesque show for the older gentleman to view at a jackshack. I—perhaps because of my hooker ass— would play the hooker who gets picked up on the street by the older gentleman. I liked my role because it was challenging. Everyone else was more or less playing themselves; I got to walk on the wild side.

The older gentleman would be played by an actor from Southern Oregon. The Pander Brothers suggested he and I meet for coffee to break the ice before our sex scene. Good idea.

We met at Kelly's Olympian for Irish coffees and got along famously. We were both well-educated and well-traveled, and so able to beat around the bush for some time. Finally I got to the point.

"So, we're supposed to have 'sex.'"

He blanched. "Yeah, I'm a bit nervous about that. The sexual activity in the rest of my scenes is all implied, but... Well, my wife is a paraplegic. I've been married for twenty-five years. I've never cheated on her once, nor has the idea ever crossed my mind. I really don't know what to expect."

"Wait a minute. You're married to a paraplegic? That's extraordinary. Good for you." I paused. "I don't know what to expect either, but I'm glad we got to chat so I know you're not a weirdo. I think at this point the only thing that'll really help is a bottle of Jack Daniels on set."

Two days later we met again in my "bedroom," a gritty place with a threadbare bed, cracked mint-green paint on the walls, a little vanity, and tons of cameras and lights. I nodded a hello to my co-star, then headed towards hair and make-up where Mona was hangin' out.

"Viva, that man you're about to fuck is hideous."

She wasn't far from wrong. I didn't answer, just pulled out my little bottle of Jack. "Trade you a swig for a cigarette," I said.

"Done."

Soon my hooker makeup was shellacked on my face and a little red wig—worn backwards and styled like Reba McEntire—pinned to my head. I slipped into my slut gear—snakeskin hot pants, see-through hot pink half-shirt, black bra and hooker fur—and grabbed my favorite kimono for a security blanket. Then I slipped into character.

I knew we weren't supposed to actually have sex, but I knew it was supposed to look like it. That meant I would have to get pretty intimate with my co-star. And I was getting paid five hundred bucks to do it. I figured that meant I *was* a prostitute. Or soft-core pornstar? What the fuck was the difference?

The crew was ready for me. We did the initial shots with both actors clothed first. Cakewalk. Then they whipped out a silicone stunt cock for me to fellate. This was during the short-lived era when porn was obsessed with safe sex. To be politically correct, the Panders wanted me to use a condom on the stunt dick. Fine. We shot several takes of me licentiously getting the condom out of the wrapper and rolling it down the dick. Then the cameras came in for a close-up and I opened wide and wrapped my throat around the silicone cock. I started choking violently.

"Cut! Cut! What's going on?" Pander seemed agitated. He probably thought he'd accidentally hired a virgin cocksucker.

I was coughing and gagging. I reached deep into my purse where I'd hidden the Jack Daniels and took a big slug of it. I almost choked on that, too.

"Jesus fucking Christ! These condoms have spermicide on them. Fucking GROSS! Any of you assholes ever tried nonoxynol-9?" I was gagging so badly I had tears in my eyes. I took another slug of Jack.

"Get her some water!" Pander barked. "I'm so sorry, Viva. It didn't occur to me that... Do you have any other condoms with you?"

"Fuck no! What do you think I am, a hooker? Call Teresa. She's got bags of those flavored ones from the county. Tell her I want banana. Whatever. I'll call. GROSS!"

We took a half hour break and fixed my smeared eye makeup, but the awful taste of the nonoxynol-9 wouldn't go away. I took a couple more slugs of the JD until finally I felt warm and ready for my sex scene.

I took off my hooker gear and wrapped my kimono tightly around me. My co-star was naked in bed, the covers pulled up to his waist. I really hoped we could nail the scene in one or two takes. I threw my robe on a chair and got under the covers with my new boyfriend.

"Quiet on set! Roll camera!"

I got on top of him. We were both fully naked, skin-on-skin. He looked terrified, but that was in keeping with his character. My character was supposed to know what the fuck she was doing. I pantomimed sex, rhythmically riding the stranger's groin, until I sensed that my co-star was developing an erection. Why hadn't anyone planned for that eventuality?

"Cut," I hollered.

"Cut. Viva, that looked great. What's the matter?" Jacob spoke softly to me, trying to maintain calm. The whole crew looked dreadfully uncomfortable.

"Can we slip a condom on this guy please? Just in case..." God, the whole thing was unbearably awkward. It would have been so much less so if we just went for it and actually had sex, rather than me sliding all over this stranger trying to mimic the act while avoiding it. It was ridiculous. For the first time in my acting career, I felt truly uncomfortable. I wanted badly for it all to be over with.

Dude put on a condom and we humped twice more for the camera before Jacob called out, "That's a wrap!"

I jumped off the bed, pulled on my kimono, and went looking for Mona for a cigarette. She was down the hall, huddled in a corner crying.

"My baby! My poor, poor baby. I'm so sorry I let you do that. You're never going to do anything like that again. I'm so sorry, Viva!"

"It's okay, mom." I was confused by her emotion. "It was just acting. It wasn't a party, but I feel okay about it. Don't worry. I'm fine."

"No, Viva. That was NOT okay. And I'll see to it that everyone apologizes to you."

"Mona, don't worry. Just give me a cigarette."

She broke down into sobs.

I had crossed some personal boundary that day, whether I wanted to admit it or not. I felt like I got a good taste of both porn and prostitution, and while that might be good for my writing, I didn't care to do either again. I wasn't ashamed of what I'd done or that it was now part of my oeuvre; I'd made other mistakes along the way—enrolling at Williams, missing my ride to the Jane's Addiction concert, forsaking my first love for the hazy promises of "the future"—but I'd learned from those mistakes and I would learn from *Suck It and See*. All the same, I wanted to make damn sure Mommy and Daddy never ever saw *Suck It*, so I invented another pseudonym to hide behind: COCO COBRA.

And there, already, is your silver lining.... Before long Coco Cobra would take on a life of her own, fronting a punk band sans clothes and yelling lyrics about sex and fighting. Before long Coco Cobra would become one of my favorite people on earth.

Changes

"Alright, Viva! You're up."

I climbed into the chair and loosed my platinum hair from the ponytail. It cascaded halfway down my back. It hadn't been this long since Africa.

"Just a trim today?"

"Paint it black," I said, surprising even myself with my certainty.

"What? Seriously?"

Paula had been trying to get me to do a dramatic change for years, but I kept resisting. The blonde hair was so much a part of my persona.

But now I felt stuck—in my relationship, in my job, in Portland. I wanted to shake things up. My hair seemed like a good place to start.

"Paint it black and chop it. Chin length. But ... uh ... would it be possible to keep a chunk of blonde up front? For nostalgia's sake?"

"Oh God, Viva, you are going to look so hot."

She gleefully retreated to the back room to mix colors. I looked at my pale countenance in the mirror. It was early December and my skin was the color of aspirin. Yes, I wanted this. Badly. A few minutes later she returned with plastic gloves on and a palette of dark gooey slime. I took a deep breath as she began to apply it.

"So what's new?"

"Absolutely nothing. Same old same old."

"You're still at Magic?"

"Yup."

"Still with Johnny?"

"Yup."

"Still got the band?"

"Yes ma'am. Actually we're playing tonight. Don't let me leave without giving you a flyer."

The band part was going well at least. After several false starts, countless basement jam sessions, and six months as a keyboard player, I finally had a band that I fronted—the Licks. I played guitar and sang and another dancer from Magic played bass. Her boyfriend and buddy rounded out the group on lead guitar and drums. She and I had worked hard over the summer, learning twelve of my songs and two of hers, plus a Sammy Davis Jr. cover, a punked-up version of Tracy Ullman's "They Don't Know," Black Sabbath's "Sweet Leaf," and Billie Holiday's "Stormy Weather." We'd already released one seven-inch and had recorded a ten-song CD. Our fan base was growing steadily and I was hard at work on new songs. Although it was a lot of work organizing and promoting shows and managing the band, I loved every minute of it. Still it couldn't cure the nonstop nausea I felt regarding my relationship.

Paula knew all about it. She'd been in charge of my hair since before I'd even met Johnny. She was there for the first blush, the crushing angst that followed fast on its heels, and the numbing dissatisfaction that had only worsened over the past two years. She had to be sick of hearing about it by now. I wasn't even gonna bring it up. Instead I promised myself I'd try to have an affair before my next appointment. Paula deserved a fresh story.

"Any plans for Christmas?"

"I'm heading home to Minnesota for a week."

"Is Johnny going along?"

"Yup. Which is actually a good thing. My parents are so in love with him that they forget to bother me. I always joke that he should date my mom."

It was true. My parents loved him. My grandmas loved him. Even cunt-face Terri at the Magic loved him. Why couldn't I? What the hell was wrong with me? Never, not once, had I felt love's delirium. Initially I thought I was broken, that the gory end of my first love affair had spoiled me forever. Still my heart kept yearning for more, and I couldn't deny it forever. But how to extricate myself? Three months before I'd had a chance, when the Lawn went condo and we were forced to move. But instead of getting a place of my own, I signed on for another tour of duty as Johnny and I moved into a lovely two-bedroom house. Why couldn't I summon the courage to fly solo? It had to be partly his fault. Everyone saw that Angel was obsessed with me, and more than a mite codependent. His last girlfriend had tricked him into moving to Portland with her, only to stay behind in Massachusetts. I knew she knew what I was feeling.... Like I'd rather jump off a bridge than continue our charade. How could Johnny not sense this? Was I that great an actress?

"Paula, why can't I just leave him? Why is it so hard? I think all the time about what I'm going to say and even schedule deadlines of when to say it. But when the time comes I simply can't do it!"

"Don't worry about it, Viva. When you're ready to make it happen you'll do it. Maybe you're one of those people who has to hit rock bottom before you make any changes. I hope for your sake you're not, but.... Let's move you to the sink."

Paula rinsed the dye out of my hair, cut off about six inches, and blow-dried it. I insisted on keeping my eyes closed the whole time.

"Okay, Viva! You're done!"

I grit my teeth and opened my eyes. I was stunned.

"Fuck yeah! Paula, you rock!"

I looked awesome. Instantly I fell in love with the girl in the mirror. It was still Viva, but edgier, punkier, more rocker. I paid my alchemist handsomely and bounced out the door with a new lease on life.

I ran a few errands and then headed home to get ready for my rock show. Johnny had prepared a Thai feast, including homemade salad rolls and vegetarian pad thai. God I am such an asshole, I thought, as Johnny toasted me by candlelight.

After dinner I slipped into my black catsuit for the show and put on my warpaint. Suddenly I didn't recognize myself. Who was this black-bobbed vixen and what had she done with Viva? My confidence crumbled.

Upset and running late, I pulled every blonde wig I owned out of storage before settling on a silver tinsel wig from the magic store. As Angel drove me across town to the Tonic Lounge, I cursed myself in silence. When had I become so weak? I couldn't break up with Johnny and now was hiding underneath a five-dollar tinsel wig! Was I so afraid of change? Would this be my new modus operandi, to plunge confidently into the cold dark unknown, only to swim frantically back to the shallow end and tread water? No way. I was going to embrace change, even if it killed me.

Two months later, on an ill-fated evening in February, I gave Johnny his walking orders and broke up my band, too. The Licks stayed broken up. But it would take two more years 'til I was desperate enough to ditch sweet Johnny for good.

Rock 'n' Roll Circus

Coco Cobra and the Killers had been together almost four months and gigging for two. My birthday was coming up at the end of July, and I wanted to throw a big birthday rock show. Johnny Angel was booking the Satyricon, so we scheduled the show there. I asked my favorite bands to be on the bill and Angel set about promoting it, laboriously

COCO COBRA & THE KILLERS

Kevin and I were getting drunk on micro-brews and MSG-filled poo-poo platters in the Magic Gardens, a seedy Chop Suey strip bar down the street from Mary's Club, when this naked girl in front of us decided to speak. She asked us to be her Johnny Thunders, and who were we to say no? She was stripping to the Stooges! Our first rehearsal was in our friend Adam's basement. He played drums. We hoped that Coco would give us a private show but she was all business, screaming and strumming her guitar. Kevin traded her some new panties for her guitar, and the Killers were born. We played our first show at another Chinese restaurant across the Willamette River. Coco's boyfriend was booking Portland's punk dive, The Satyricon, so we played there, and we played at the Russian strip bar, Union Jacks, and the former strip bar, EJ's. During this time we were playing quite a few shows with a great band called the Pills. They took us into their basement for a few days and recorded the 12 songs on this disc. I sent the disc out to some record labels hoping to get back a few boxes of colored vinyl 7"s to sell at shows for beer money, but that never happened. When Adam died last year I dug out the CD and made a few copies for people who knew him. If you were around to see the naked drunken mess of Coco Cobra and the Killers, then you'll remember these sex tunes. If you weren't, this is what it was like in Portland, OR in 1999, but with Chinese Food and strippers.

- Jesse, New York City 2004

the "I NEED SEX" sessions

photocopying, cutting, and pasting images of all my rock 'n' roll heroes for the poster.

The day of the show I packed Coco's wig and boots in a duffel bag, and slipped into a micro-minidress for my birthday meet-and-greet. I ran up Burnside, cars honking at my ass, to the Crystal Ballroom to say hello to the boys from the Jon Spencer Blues Explosion and Andre "Jailbait" Williams. Both the JSBE and Andre had sat for interviews with me for *Exotic* and we'd kept in touch and developed a friendship. They put me on the VIP guest list that night so I could hang out with them backstage before our respective shows.

Andre Williams was a contemporary of Ike and Tina Turner and was dubbed "Mr. Rhythm." He'd fallen on hard times in the eighties and nineties, something to do with drugs and women. The Demolition Doll Rods found him on the streets of Detroit, backed him in the studio, and now his career was back from the dead after the release of *Silky*, the nastiest, most stripperific album of 1998.

Andre welcomed me like a daughter in his little dressing room. He was wearing a tracksuit and complaining bitterly that all his pimp suits had been stolen on tour. That meant he had to wear a sailor outfit to do his shtick, which I had to admit was pretty ridiculous. Still, Andre had the *cojones* to pull off even that.

I peeked in on the JSBE and was promptly handed a beer. I knew I had to get back to the 'Con, so I kissed 'em all twice, slammed the beer, and headed back down Burnside, but not without insisting that all of them come to my birthday bash.

Back at the Satyricon, the first band was just finishing up. I grabbed my duffel bag and morphed into Coco Cobra in the filthy bathroom. Wig, red lipstick, boots, and off with the dress! From then on I stalked around the rock club wearing nothing but a PVC t-back and biker jacket.

Around midnight, Coco Cobra and the Killers took the stage. Our thirteen-song set lasted approximately twenty minutes, and included such garage-punk insta-classics as "I Need Sex" and "I Hate You." The club was packed, hot and sweaty. People were dancing and throwing beer, slipping and sliding and making out in doorways. Midway through the show, I caught a glimpse of a tall black man in a sailor suit walking through the front door, accompanied by Jon Spencer, Russell

Simins, and Judah Bauer. The rock stars had made it to my birthday party!

Andre walked all the way up to the stage to give me a kiss. I motioned for him to come onstage.

"Ladies and Gentleman, may I introduce Andre fucking Williams! Mr. Rhythm himself!"

I convened briefly with the Killers. What song could we whip out that Andre might know? We decided to try "Louie, Louie." Andre didn't appear to be familiar with it, but danced licentiously and improvised hilarious lyrics. Just when the song started getting really out of control, Mona appeared in the back of the crowded bar, rollerskating towards the stage and carrying a huge cake that was on fire with twenty-five candles.

"Happy Birthday to you!"

This song at least Andre knew. The crowd parted for Mona. She was good on skates, but was also clearly wasted. Somehow she managed to climb the stairs to the stage with the cake still upright. She was mere inches from me when the inevitable finally happened: she tripped on a guitar cord and the cake went flying. Coco squealed with glee, but poor Mr. Rhythm looked horrified. He rocked back and forth on his feet, shell-shocked. He was a professional musician from a different era, and you could see his mind working as he wondered how he was going to finesse the situation.

But Coco knew what to do. As the band launched into "I Wanna Be With You Tonight," she grabbed a fistful of cake and fed it to Andre suggestively. Then she grabbed another handful, smeared it on her breasts, and let the female revelers in the front row lick it off while she was singing.

The band finished the set with a cover, "Have Love, Will Travel," and their theme song, "Coco Cobra and the Killers." By the end there was cake and beer all over everyone and the vintage Farfisa keyboard had taken a stage dive and hit the floor.

I was in heaven. Finally I had a band that I loved; I loved the music and I loved my bandmates. Every time we got together was a literal riot. And now my own heroes had witnessed me in action. If this was any indication of how my twenty-fifth year was going to go, I could die happy before I turned twenty-six! And ideally I would die before twenty-six.

Somehow twenty-six seemed loaded with foreboding, piled with imperatives to grow-the-fuck-up, haunted by early echoes of the ticking biological clock. If I was going to kick a hole in Portland's ceiling, it had to be now. Twenty-five. Then I'd go straight. Promise.

* * *

My birthday show at the 'Con was Mona's final appearance. She'd had it with Portland by then. Or, rather, she was sick of her codependent relationship with Lucian. His enabling her by paying for everything ultimately paralyzed her. She hadn't produced much of anything in over a year, and her self-esteem was at rock bottom. A week after my birthday she left for Sturgis to bartend during the biker rally. When she came back three weeks later, it was just to get her stuff.

It was then that some wallet she'd been flirting with bought her a kick-ass pair of red cowboy boots, boots made for walkin' out on Lucian, boots that symbolized her future in Butte, Montana. She'd been asked to be on a board of directors of the Dumas Brothel Restoration Project, an international resource for sex workers housed in a former brothel. I couldn't believe she was deserting. She seemed so self-possessed about it that I felt horribly betrayed. Didn't she love us and need us? Was she even going to say goodbye?

She did say goodbye. A few of us met at Hung Far Low—as good a place as any for this kind of wake—to bid her adieu. Afterward Lucian and Mona drove me home. As we turned up my street, Mona started sobbing.

"Viva, I'm so proud of you. You've done more in this town than I ever could. You're amazing. Be strong. Don't ever forget how much I love you."

I was shocked. It may have been the first nice thing Mona had ever said to me. I choked up.

"Oh, Mom! Why do you have to go? I can't do it without you!"

"Yes you can, Viva. You've been doing it by yourself this whole time."

"Bullshit. I'm following you out of here. Watch me."

"GO, Viva. Get out of the car. This hurts too fucking much."

I got out of the car and hollered after it as it turned down Sherman

Street. "Good luck, Mom. I'll be wishing on stars for you. Watch out, Montana!"

And she vanished. Once again I had the feeling that Mona was better at living my own destiny than I was. I was the one who wanted out, wanted more, and now she'd beaten me to the punch. Of course my career was nothing like hers; she was mysterious and mercurial. I was reliable as the rain. I showed up early for my regular stripping shifts, my columns and interviews appeared every month in *Exotic*, and I could be counted on for at least two outrageous solo shows a year. It pissed me off. I wanted to be mysterious and mercurial for a change. Or maybe I just wanted a change.

Jesus Christ, Part Two

It has been my experience that the universe is indeed quite responsive to prayer. Like say you're really fucking fed-up with your lover, your life, your everything. As with saying you're an alcoholic, just being able to iterate your situation is the first step towards changing it, and that is what prayer is. That and trust that some force—even if it's just the force of iteration—is set in motion thereby.

That same summer, shortly after Mona hit the road, I returned to my Minnesota headwaters to welcome my friend Heather's new baby. Heather and I were as different as could be. She was an evangelical Christian, a Republican, and pro-life. I was constitutionally opposed to all those things. However, in the remote northern wilderness where we met, we seemed to have more in common than not. We were best friends throughout high school and remained close through college. That she was married by twenty and would have five kids by thirty never fazed me, and my stripping never fazed her. As long as we avoided the topics of religion, politics, and abortion, we got along famously.

My trip to the woods was cleansing. I went alone, leaving Angel to minister to the cats, and serendipitously arrived in my hometown of Grand Marais with "The Storm of the Century" at my heels.

If you get to witness a Storm of the Century without getting your ass killed, it's truly a magnificent thing. Nature is a motherfucker, and she was in quite a mood that night. She was deceptively languid in the early evening, the air soft and warm, the sky a riot of color. But around midnight, an electrical storm lit up the heavens. Then came the winds. Hundred milers that scoured the hills, tore down buildings, and ripped up trees. I sat on my ex-boyfriend's porch, gazing out over Good Harbor Hill. The storm was a veritable blitzkrieg, dozens of tongues of electricity knifing the night at any given moment. The ex and I drank whiskey from a bottle and talked about love and not-love, pausing occasionally for a nostalgic kiss. The voltage in the air was palpable, and I realized how long I'd been missing it: in my relationship, in my cozy Portland life, in its stagnant weather systems that never so much as grumbled with thunder, much less mercilessly scoured the earth.

The next morning dawned bright and clear with the power out for miles. Trees were down everywhere. Roads were blocked. The whole county was a mess, but my insides felt cleaner than they'd been since I moved to Portland. All the booze, the boy, the weather had put me to sleep. Now I was awake.

That afternoon I met with another girlfriend of mine, a crazy artist with an occasional propensity towards evangelism. She led me in prayer in her Jeep Cherokee after I spilled my guts and told her I was starving for change, desperate to come unmoored from the boy and the bar. I needed so much more. So we asked for more, and that I have assistance in making the necessary maneuvers to extricate myself from proto-yuppie faux-bliss and find my path again.

Two short months later, it appeared my prayers had been answered.

Movie Star

"You've got an amazing face. Do you ever do any acting?"

I'd heard it a million times before. "What do you think this is?" I shot back, my "amazing face" peering back at him, upside down, from between my naked legs.

"We're shooting a trailer in town over the next couple months and you'd be perfect in it. Could we maybe arrange a screen test?"

"Of course. But first you're taking me out for a drink."

"You got it. Here's my number."

His name was Lyon, a director who had recently returned to America from Germany. He'd lived in Portland for many years and was back to shoot a feature he'd written about a stripper and her boyfriend who get entangled with crooked cops. There was very generous financing for the teaser trailer, which upon completion would be shopped around to big Hollywood studios. Hollywood would love it, throw millions at it, we'd shoot the feature and soon be rich and famous. Sounded good to me!

I aced my screen test and was cast as the stripper, the female lead. Abruptly my shoulds evaporated. Lyon was legitimate and, judging by his successful career in Europe, his future looked bright. Suddenly so did mine. During the days I worked amongst the film community, a vibrant and close-knit family. On the nights I wasn't working I'd find myself at an ostentatious feast or party, hosted by a gentleman named Paul and attended by Portland's gritty downtown music crowd and a few fancier hangers-on. Lyon was close friends with Paul, an LA producer who made millions off a popular reality TV show he'd created. Paul lived in Portland so that his two sons could grow up grounded in someplace that wasn't LA, but still traveled there frequently to get his hair cut, see his therapist, and buy his custom snakeskin pants. Perhaps he had a touch of guilt about his conspicuous wealth, because he loved nothing more than showering it on us starving artists. He fed us and occasionally fostered us. He was generous to a fault, fun-loving and brilliant. When he came into the Magic Gardens, he tipped hundreds rather than singles. Occasionally he'd buy a round for the entire bar.

Wait a minute. Was I a starving artist? I had plenty of cash on hand, it's true, and a couple grand ferreted away for the trip to Morocco I dreamed of taking. But I was still paying off college loans and other debts, making frequent visits to the naturopath to keep my depression at bay, and finally realizing that Goodwill wasn't the fashion emporium I always thought it was. Though I made piles of cash four nights a week, there was always somewhere for it to go. Like most strippers I knew, I was living hand to mouth. When Paul started coming regularly to the Magic Gardens, it was like we all got a raise.

I was thrilled about my new friends and new job opportunities. I had fresh hope for the future and felt like I was going in the right direction. Mom and Dad were happy, too—acting presented a healthy alternative to strip clubs, even if they might have preferred I join the Foreign Service.

Serendipity was in my court again, it seemed. Just when I started to feel the first twinges of stripper burnout, a tantalizing new path appeared. The rest of my little clique was moving on as well. Rain had left the stage months ago and given birth to a beautiful baby boy. Pink had finally ditched the jackshacks and was working full-time at the university. Mona sent the occasional postcard from Montana, where she had happily become a fixture at the M&M Bar on Butte's main drag, and Teresa's nonprofit was off to a fabulous start. In fact, Teresa was currently organizing a rag-tag team of sex workers to storm City Hall, and was about to make history.

I Fought the Law

It was late October. My deadline at the magazine had just wrapped, and I was enjoying my first day off in weeks. I'd stripped the night before; every single muscle was sore—my back, my fingers, my ears—so I swam thirty laps to stretch out. As I was leaving the gym, a few cool drops of rain started to fall. The suits on lunch break yelped with

SCARLET LETTER

The Scarlet Letter is a collective of workers fighting the recent Portland City Ordinance concerning personal models and escorts.

glee and stepped outside to feel the rain on their faces. Portland had been enjoying an extra-long Indian summer and it seemed like it hadn't rained in six months. It was refreshing and comforting to see it rain, reminding all of us that we were in Portland and that the cozy, slower-paced winter months loomed ahead.

I pulled my floppy black velvet hat down to my eyes and turned down Alder Street for the three-block walk to Teresa's office. She'd been working her ass off, traveling to Amsterdam, Scotland, and Philadelphia to strip and to New Mexico, Florida, and Minnesota for conferences on harm reduction and needle exchange. Back at home her star was really taking off: the county had approached her for help with its street outreach programs, paying her for her expertise and inspiring her to seek out more public funds. She'd become an expert grant writer and *Danzine* was now a legitimate nonprofit with an actual office and a platoon of volunteers. The zine's publication schedule had dwindled to perhaps once a year, but Teresa's greater cause—saving the world (or at least the more fucked-up bottom strata of it)—was progressing nicely.

I walked into the elegant lobby of the Washington/Park Building and took the elevator to the fourth floor. Teresa's corner office was at the end of a long hall, past offices of architects and attorneys. My, how we'd come up in the world!

Her office was big. There was an enormous desk in the corner covered with all her various works-in-progress. Another desk was set up with a donated computer, printer, and scanner. Teresa wasn't good with computers and so recruited interns from Portland State University to build her website and keep track of e-mails. Old metal office shelves lined the back wall, stocked with stacks of back issues of *Danzine*, grant writing how-to books, clear storage bins filled with condoms (male and female), dental dams and lube, clean syringes, and feminine hygiene supplies. A large Free Box near the door was filled with donated clothes, everything from stripper stuff to sweaters and socks. The walls were covered with art, much of it inspired or commissioned by Teresa.

"Hey, V! Get caught in the rain?" Teresa said as she hugged me, feeling my wet coat.

"It's drizzling. Everyone's overjoyed. How's the war?"

"Dude, we're in full battle mode. This City Council fight is gonna be huge. The escorts are terrified; so terrified they're actually showing up to our meetings. We've got feminist groups onboard, several concerned mothers and a grandma. Even the Wobblies are throwin' down. It's totally awesome."

A bill had been railroaded through the Council chambers two months before, requiring that every escort and lingerie model register with the cops—a two-hundred-dollar fee. Each worker would be required to carry a permit on her person stating her real name, address, and other vital stats. Every guy and girl in the biz was terrified. The city claimed it was trying to regulate an industry of independent contractors, but these new scarlet letters that betrayed identities and home addresses put workers in peril. Furthermore, why did the guys and gals have to register with the cops as if they were criminals? Most independent contractors registered with the city. There was a lot wrong with the whole thing, not least of all the fact that the bill had been passed without any of the usual public discussion or debate. The city obviously didn't think that escorts and lingerie models would fight back. The city obviously hadn't met Teresa.

Most escorts in *Exotic Magazine* and *Willamette Week* advertised "Full Service." In laymen's terms this generally meant intercourse or, as some called it, prostitution. Lingerie modeling studios were oftentimes fronts for prostitution as well. In the studios, a guy hired a girl to model for him privately while he jacked off. The advertised forty-dollar show meant the model was eight feet away. For twenty bucks more she'd be four feet away. Throw a hundred at her and who knows what would happen. Much was negotiable in these private rooms with minimal security or surveillance. Of course the Mayor's office wanted to crack down on the blatant disregard of Portland's prostitution laws, but it was expensive and ineffectual for the vice squad to go after each escort. There were occasional stings, but police preferred to prey on streetwalkers. The new ordinance threatened the livelihood of every escort and lingerie model. More importantly to Teresa, the ordinance seriously endangered their lives.

"I ran everything past my attorney and he says we're good to go. The Council hasn't followed procedure at all. They were planning to slip this through without anyone noticing."

Teresa never said one way or another whether she actually "traded"— i.e., sex for money—but she bought a small ad in *Exotic* every month

158

advertising a "Quality Foot Rub" and I knew her to be familiar with lots of hotel lobbies. She also had an attorney on retainer who would defend her—for free—on grounds of civil disobedience should she ever get busted (though for what she never said). I admired this so much. I had no intention of trading actual sex for money, but I always tried to follow Teresa's lead and be vague about it. That way I could be a spokesperson for the larger sex industry—the trannies, pornstars, phone sex operators, escorts, streetwalkers, and lingerie models—as well as the untouchable all-nude girls who thought themselves apart from and above the rest. As I saw it, we were all equally vulnerable as part of the invisible fringe, and when the powers that be picked on one of us, we all took a hit. We needed unity.

"So what do you want from me?" I asked Teresa.

"We want you to be there. Council starts at 9 AM. Doors open at eight thirty. We want to pack the place. Of course, if you'd like to donate your voice…." She purred, turning on the temptress, dropping her businesslike demeanor and flashing her megawatt toothy smile. There are a lot of valuable lessons to be learned in the sex industry, and Teresa had always been at the head of the class.

"Sure. I'd love to speak. What do you want me to say? I can write something…"

"We're giving everybody their lines. Because Council rules strictly limit floor time to two minutes per person, we have to carefully choreograph our presentation to make sure we get to say everything we want to say. We have to register a week in advance, too, so we need to know exactly who's gonna say what when."

"I'll be there with bells on and I'll say whatever you want me to say. Teresa, you kick so much fuckin' ass I wanna buy you a new pair of steel-toed boots."

She cackled loudly as she ran to get the phone. I flipped through a stack of zines on the coffee table and kicked back on the enormous Victorian couch near the window. It was Morgan Le Fay's couch. She'd had it reupholstered in pomegranate velvet before giving it to Teresa for the office. Morgan was making serious money "trading." She rented her own studio up the street where she saw a handful of regular clients. She spent much of her downtime volunteering for *Danzine*.

God, Teresa had awesome zines lying around. Her appetite for them was insatiable, and she had some real gems. There were several pro-union zines, horrific tell-alls by temp workers and office slaves, several colorful comic books including Teresa's favorite, *Love and Rockets*, and a black-and-white twenty-page zine called *Sharp*, featuring a drawing of a syringe on the cover. The last one really caught my eye: it was a pro-addiction treatise written by a heroin junkie. In it she detailed the daily humiliations of searching for the stuff, wrote a couple paeans to junk, reviewed a handful of records, and made a plea for a more enlightened way of thinking about addiction. Hey, junkies have rights, too! Just because they got hooked on an illicit substance rather than alcohol, sugar, sex, or money didn't meant they should be ostracized as hopeless pariahs.

Once again my brain stretched a little further to accommodate a new strain of activism while my heart swelled with admiration for Teresa. She was impossibly beautiful, fearless, energetic, and smart. Was she a junkie, too? Who knew. Who cared. She was unstoppable, and the City of Portland would soon find out.

Teresa was still on the phone, repeating the City Council spiel. From what I could overhear, she was talking to one of the local media. She turned to me and mouthed "Five more minutes." I shrugged my shoulders. I had time to kill before my four o'clock cocktail date, and what better way to kill it than flipping through Teresa's mind-blowing library?

There was a knock at the door. Morgan.

"VIVA! How are you?" She said in a loud, singsong voice.

Morgan looked great. She'd put on a lot of weight—probably forty pounds since Terri had fired her from the Magic for being "too fat"— and looked marvelously curvy and luxurious. She loved her work as a lady of leisure. She was absolutely glowing.

"I just came by to drop off flyers for the Masquerade Ball. I've got some for you, too. It's really just a big huge party for us, but invite whomever you want—it's also a fundraiser for the magazine. From five to twenty dollars, sliding scale. Two bucks off with a can of food."

"I can't wait," I replied. "Masquerade Balls are so kinky. My band's getting really tight, too. I think we'll be ready. But how are you? How's life? How's work? How's Billy?"

Morgan always had a hot little boy-girl by her side. The latest was thin and lanky like a skateboarder, had a husky voice, and wore his crewcut blonde and spiked.

"Life's great. Work is awesome. Billy is a dream. Really, I love my work—everything about it. I've always wanted to be bigger and now I can be whatever size I want. And the johns are just crazy about my weight. I have a handful of regulars and I'm making three times as much as I did as a stripper. My studio is right up the street and I can take public transportation to get there. It's decorated like a late-19th-century brothel. And you know who's right upstairs? Tanya. She got a studio in my building."

"Tanya trades now, too, doesn't she? Doesn't anyone get suspicious? You hot chicks coming and going with all sorts of different men?"

"Nah. It's real private. Actually I was going to invite you over to my place for a photo shoot/interview session. This TV show in Florida somehow caught wind of what we're doing up here and this woman— Margot is her name—wants to interview Viva Las Vegas."

"Jesus. When it rains it pours!"

I was shooting a movie, I had a new band in addition to Coco Cobra and the Killers, I was performing solo acoustic gigs, the City Hall thing promised to be high-profile, and now I was going to be appearing on a TV show in Florida? I needed a manager! "Everyone wants a piece of us! At least you're getting paid for it. Hey, I was gonna ask you… how does Billy handle your job?"

"It's a total nonissue. We're lesbians. If some man wants to put his hands all over me or have sex with me, it's a job. I'm sure if I had women clients it would be harder on him. He actually gets jealous when I dance for dykes at the Egyptian Room. But for me to entertain a man—even sexually—is completely non-threatening."

One was always to use masculine pronouns for Morgan's lovers, even though they were clearly women. It had taken me a while to get the hang of this.

"Hey, Morgan! What's up?" Teresa was finally off the phone.

"Hey honey. I brought you some posters and handbills for the Ball. I'll do a big press release next week."

"Dude, we are so going to deserve that party when we're done with the Mayor's office. That was the *Oregonian* on the phone. They'll be in the house when we crash the Council meeting. We'll invite them to cover the Masquerade Ball, too."

"Good idea. Viva's new band is gonna play."

"Really? What's your new band, V?"

"Viva and Four Hot Guys," I deadpanned. "We don't have a name yet, but it's the best band I've ever had. We fuckin' rock. We're working on a T. Rex cover right now. It's so hot."

My new boys were all veteran musicians who'd loved the Licks. Although Coco Cobra and the Killers was deliriously fun, the music was strictly garage rock. Our set of snotty songs about sex left no room for the poppier tunes I'd penned for my former band. Plus Coco's hands were always too busy with obscene gestures to play guitar. I really missed playing guitar. The new guys convinced me that my songs deserved an audience, and offered to back me up. Our debut would be Morgan's First Annual Sex Workers' Masquerade Ball and I wanted it to be unforgettable.

Morgan giggled. "Viva and Four Hot Guys is a swell name for a band. Wish I'd known; I would've put it on the flyers."

I looked at the clock. It was five minutes to four.

"Shit! I've gotta run. I'm meeting my co-star at Kelly's Olympian. Lyon thinks it'd be good if we at least get to know each other before we fall in love on camera. I hope he's hot. I'm really not up for a repeat of *Suck It…*"

I grabbed a handful of condoms and kissed Morgan and Teresa on each cheek.

"I'll call you with your lines by this weekend!" Teresa hollered after me as I ran down the hall.

* * *

I FOUGHT THE LAW
"The Gospel According to Viva Las Vegas"
(Exotic Magazine, *December 1999)*

GODDAMN I love this town!! Portland sex workers RULE!!

Just when I was feeling another Christmas poem swelling within me, Portland sex workers stunned me into absolute evangelism. AGAIN!

Only three hungover days after our fabulous Sex Workers Masquerade Ball, City Council met to discuss their recently minted City ordinance 14.44 that requires lingerie models and escorts to obtain expensive permits after invasive identification procedures. (If you're not hip to this and have ever tried to join the FBI or CIA, well, becoming a Pornland model or escort is now harder than that.)

Ordinance 14.44 passed without any of the usual public discussion or input back in September. That said, it wasn't up for debate at all. It was probably just a matter of antiquated decorum that saw Ordinance 14.44 on the agenda at all, tacked on last as it was. However, a motley crew of nearly thirty of Portland's most invisible population, her sex workers, roused themselves by 8 AM to sit through a long Council meeting where they were treated rather dismissively, but in the end surprised everyone, even themselves, with their display of unity, intelligence, and passion.

Alongside us were friends, musicians, and leaders of local feminist organizations. It was heartening just to feel that somehow the word got out to our various communities, although the Ordinance was railroaded through the council without so much as a peep of dissent or media awareness. Even by the time of the November meeting, the council members seemed to have forgotten that they routed the constitution a short month before and fucked over a large part of the local economy. (Hey, Mayor Katz! You know how you wanna draw conventions and their bundles of cash to Pornland? What do conventioneers want besides a nice hotel room and good public transportation?! WHORES!! You idiot.)

When we finally got our chance to speak, sixteen women spoke concisely and eloquently for two minutes each on issues ranging from public health, domestic abuse, child safety issues, and privacy of workers and their clients, to, of course, the truly demonizing nature of the law and its blatant unfairness.

My point then, and now, is that it is impossible to legislate the sex industry out of existence. Prostitutes always have existed and they always will. The sex industry represents as much as a quarter of our GNP, and 85% of the world wide web. Now, why would you want to go back in time and ghettoize a group of largely self-employed, entrepreneurial women who are mindful of safety issues? Ordinance 14.44 will put more illicit activity back on Portland's streets, where it is harder to keep track of or regulate. Now that the issue is on the drawing board, let it be in keeping with Portland's supposedly long and proud tradition of progressive, community-informed and community-positive legislation. Instead of taking two steps back by demonizing this large population, take a step forward with progressive legislation that would ensure that the sex industry is a safe, law-abiding organization that guarantees its workers rights and its clients privacy. Next time you make sweeping ordinances that affect a large part of the voting populace, ask them first what they want, what they need, and what their concerns are. Is that inconceivable? Vera Katz, this is no Third Reich. Saddling sex workers with gold stars or scarlet letters does nothing for team spirit.

Meanwhile, I'm still embarrassed to be living in a country where, after one hundred years as voting citizens, women STILL can't use their bodies as they wish. Why can we accept money for getting fucked in pornography or Hollywood, or for offering our sexual organs up for sale (i.e., uterus, eggs, brain), but not when we, the WOMAN, are solely in charge of the decision? Our government is pimping us! It's untenable! My philosophy is if you see a sister getting fucked unfairly, you yell rape and fuckin' fight it! I'm YELLING.

P.S. Kudos to Commissioner Charlie Hales for showing us girls respect and for complimenting me on my testimony. You are dreamy, Commissioner Hales.

P.P.S. Viva's new Band!! Satyricon December 12th. Winner of the "Name Viva's Band" contest gets one night with the band member of his/her choice!! Also, Viva acoustic same night around the corner at the Milk Bar. Happy Holidays!

Trouble

The month of November had been portentous. We fought City Hall and won and my new band had pulled off a stellar debut. We'd finished shooting the trailer for Lyon's film, and the dailies looked fantastic. I'd also fallen in love.

It happened the night of the Masquerade Ball. I was dressed

regally for the event in a floor-length vintage slip, which I'd dyed royal blue, and a matching electric-blue Marie Antoinette wig, heaped with long fat ringlets. I wore a butterfly mask and vintage pink satin heels, decorated with elaborately rhinestoned butterfly brooches. My band—which now had a name: the Killboys—appeased me by wearing skinny black suits with even skinnier black ties à la Blondie. Our short, five-song set was well-rehearsed; the only thing I had to be nervous about was the striptease aria I was doing to kick off our act.

I mingled and flirted and posed for photos. Ladies of the night absolutely love to dress up, so there were plenty of peacocks around, spreading their feathers. The man who would be my ruin didn't even recognize me, although he'd seen me in every state of undress on the film shoot. I hadn't thought much of him during the filming; he seemed a pompous bastard to me. He was a friend of Lyon's, a screenwriter who deigned to help out on crew. He was a handsome, brilliant scofflaw. He had a name, but I called him Trouble.

When it came time for the Killboys to take the stage, I summoned Pink to my side and gave him his props. He was in full Mr. Pink attire: black suit, tie and hat, plus a sexy black cat mask. His task was to play butler while I sang the aria, and to assist me as I dressed in my rocker get-up after I stripped out of my gown. This was a cakewalk as far as a Mr. Pink performance went; the last cabaret he'd been recruited to assist Teresa with lube and logistics as she demonstrated for the crowd how to use a female condom. Poor Mr. Pink almost always got his hands dirty in the line of duty.

The band was in place with their backs to the audience. Pink escorted me on his arm to center stage.

"Good evening, ladies and gentlemen," I purred. "Tonight I have prepared something special for you. An aria by Wolfgang Amadeus Mozart."

Berbati's Pan was a large venue and was packed to capacity. The room suddenly fell silent. Fuck! I couldn't believe I was doing this. Singing opera naked. The punk rockers might not get it. And if I didn't start breathing soon there was no way I'd be able to pull it off.

I gave a little dramatic hiss into the mic, trying to summon some feline lassitude, some devil-may-care. It worked. I was in character.

"Giunse alfin il momento!"

My clear soprano ricocheted off the walls of the venue. *"Deh Vieni! Non Tardar"* was my favorite aria—a challenging one from *The Marriage of Figaro*—and I loved singing it. I clocked the audience mischievously as I sang, and couldn't help but notice their open mouths and wide eyes. They were terrified.

Slowly I began peeling off my dress. Once I had it over my breasts, it slid down my hips to the floor. I stood there naked, singing my little heart out for a full minute. Then Pink took two steps towards me and held out my costume change.

"Vieni ove amore per goder t'apella…"

I continued to sing as I slipped on the black leather miniskirt and black biker jacket. I zipped the jacket up slowly, halfway, then climbed into my leopard platform shoes. Pink turned towards my amp and fetched my beautiful blond-on-blond Stratocaster. He helped me strap it on, ceremoniously handed me a pick, bowed slightly, then exited the stage. The Killboys turned around in unison to face the audience. I played the opening bars to T. Rex's "Twentieth Century Boy," and all those gaping mouths spread sideways into grins. I'd pulled it off!

When I saw Trouble again later that night, he knew damn well who I was. And he had a look in his eye that could only be one thing: deadly, damning, eat-your-heart-out, fuck-your-life-up love.

9 1/2 Weeks

Falling in love is much like a car accident. It's always inconvenient, almost always painful, and frequently fatal. That people wish to fall in love always seemed idiotic to me. "I wish to be paralyzed in a terrible accident." Maybe it's for the drugs. Those first three months are the best drug on earth.

I have no idea what happened after the night of the Masquerade Ball. I don't know how my affair with Trouble started or who started it. I don't think I regained consciousness for a month, and then realized I was in the midst of a holocaust, my life in flames about me. I didn't give a damn who cried, cared, or died. I was already planning the next part, the phoenix rising from the ashes bit. I guess this sort of cataclysm is what I'd been hoping for. I wasn't expecting that the whole affair would drive me insane.

Trouble was a romantic by nature. Black Irish and all poet, he courted me as if his life and reputation depended on it. He was chivalrous, too. Sex was o-u-t until I was single, so instead we indulged in epic make-out sessions under highway overpasses, whispered vows along the train tracks, nuzzled in culverts and on stoops all over Old Town. He was everything Johnny was not; he lived by his wits, had a healthy criminal mind, was wise instead of smart, was a gypsy. He was also an extraordinary classical guitarist who wrote songs for me that made me weep.

Trouble showed me that there was indeed a way out of Portland and away from Johnny. The whiff of freedom was irresistible and I fantasized about how I'd follow him to San Francisco or Paris or New York where we would subsist on the succor of our new love indefinitely.

Meanwhile my relationship with Johnny was chugging along predictable as ever. We were heading to Minnesota again for Christmas, and he was intimating that he'd bought me a very big present. Hoping that it wasn't an engagement ring, I did a bit of detective work. It didn't take much: a couple intercepted phone calls from a piano hospital and I had a pretty good idea that the sweetheart had bought me a piano, something I'd wanted for years.

It seemed like the perfect metaphor. Although Johnny was wonderfully adept at grounding me, he wanted me to stay grounded. I was aching to fly. Trouble knew how to fly; his feet never touched the ground. Soon I knew I would have to choose: the piano or the music. The nest or the sky.

Don't Look Back

The century was gasping its last breath. Some said so was civilization. I didn't care. I was ready to go. My cards were all played and I was reasonably satisfied with the outcome. Truth is, I had no idea what to do next. I'd milked the naked girl thing as much as I cared to, my bands had played every venue in town, I had written as many diatribes as I needed to write, and I was deeply in love with someone who wasn't my boyfriend, perhaps the most reckless feeling in the world. It would save me a lot of agony if the world ended. I wouldn't have to look for a new career or break up with Johnny Angel. I wouldn't have to pay my Visa bill or January rent. That would be great.

Still, just in case the world didn't end, the Volvo was getting an oil change while Paula touched up my roots at the salon. Angel was already in Duluth with my parents. He'd waited too long to buy his plane tickets and so had to leave before me. Tonight I had the house to myself. Maybe I'd have Trouble over. But first I was gonna see *Don't Look Back*, the Dylan biopic by D. A. Pennebaker that was playing at Cinema 21. Then I'd pack and, in the morning, fly home for Christmas.

Physically I was burned out. My affair was eating up all my free time and the terrible lurchings of my heart were making it impossible to sleep. My deadline at the magazine was early because of the holidays, and I'd been doing film work while fronting Coco Cobra and the Killers as well as the Killboys. The only thing that brought in any real money was stripping and, with five shifts a week, I was getting burned out on that, too.

Spiritually I was exhausted. Something had to change. Trouble wanted me to move with him anywhere else and collaborate on screenplays. He made plenty of money doing that, and assured me I would as well. Lyon was promising me a hot new movie career. Another film had already cast me as the lead and was scheduled to start shooting in March. If just one of these things panned out, I'd be sprung from Portland and dancing and wouldn't have to think about what came next for another few years.

I hoped the Dylan movie would revive me. With all my running around, I didn't have time for dinner, so I grabbed a shot and a handful of cocktail nuts at the bar next to the movie theater. I couldn't wait to feast my eyes on young Dylan's visage for two hours, to hear his awesome music and be inspired by his rebelliousness and integrity. Maybe I could take a cue from him. After the concert at Royal Albert Hall, Dylan disappeared, torched his career, and became even more enigmatic. Sounded like a plan. Don't look back. Look forward.

The lights went down, I made it through the previews, then promptly fell asleep.

End of the World

Getting Coco dressed is a snap. The hardest thing about it, really, is making sure the little pieces of black electrical tape I use to cover her nipples are approximately the same size. Then it's just a leather G-string, long black wig, a handful of bobby pins and my knee-high seven-inch platform black leather boots and *voilà!* Coco Cobra!

It was New Year's Eve and Coco Cobra and the Killers were playing the Satyricon to usher in the new millennium. This was a big honor, but also something of a gamble. The City of Portland, braced for a Y2K meltdown, had made it virtually impossible for anyone to get downtown. No traffic was allowed other than public transportation, and riot cops (the ones who tend to incite riots) were everywhere. Angel was at work, so I pulled on some riot gear of my own—black velvet leggings, a black cashmere turtleneck, and a three-quarter-length hooker fur—raccoon lined with leopard—and marched in my boots to the bus stop.

Sure enough, the 'Con was empty. Only homeless junkies had bothered to show up, probably just to get out of the cold December rain. The opening band stalled as long as they could, hoping in vain that some kind of audience might materialize. We stalled, too, and halfway through our set my dozen-plus movie friends arrived in Paul's two big black Cadillac Escalades. Paul was an honorary cop, a result of the

COCO COBRA & THE KILLERS

SATYRICON 12·31·99
LAST NIGHT ON EARTH

fealty inspired amongst the boys in blue by Paul's reality TV show, so I wasn't surprised they'd managed to get past the roadblocks. Coco was thrilled to see him: Paul traveled with at least two bodyguards at all times, something Coco loved. That way she could mouth off to anyone, something Viva'd never do.

Trouble was there, but Coco didn't know what to do with him. Viva didn't mind pussy-whipped little sycophants; she rather liked them. To Coco they were just a fuckin' pain in the fuckin' ass.

The band finished at a quarter 'til midnight. Paul had bought twenty hundred-dollar tickets to the swell New Year's event at Union Station, so everyone squeezed into the Escalades for the five-block drive down 6th Avenue to ring in the new year amongst the cake eaters.

The gritty turn-of-the-century train station had been polished like Cinderella and was swarming with swans in black tie. Coco stood out like Dorothy in Oz with her black leather boots and drag-queen hair and make-up. She had no problem amassing admirers and free drinks, but Trouble was stalking her. She needed space. She told him she was headed for the can, then headed for the stage instead. The band finished their song and started the countdown.

"Five! Four! Three!"

Coco chanted with 'em. "TWO!! ONE!!!!"

And there was Teresa, at the stroke of midnight, ravishing in a silver snakeskin ball gown. Coco stuck her tongue down Teresa's throat, came up for air and shouted, "Here's to OUR millennium!"

"VIVA!" Teresa hollered as her date materialized with fresh champagne for the three of them.

Suddenly Trouble appeared out of nowhere, furious at having missed his New Year's kiss.

"I'm so sorry, darling. I was looking everywhere for you. You were nowhere to be found!" said Coco, doing her best Viva Las Vegas imitation.

Trouble grabbed her by the arm and steered her outside. Coco was not happy with this gesture. Her eyes gleamed yellow as the two of them argued under the awning for the length of a cigarette. Trouble was deeply wounded. Why was she ignoring him? Didn't she love him anymore?

Coco didn't want a scene. She held her cards close to her chest.

Grinning like a Cheshire cat, she said, "Of course I love you baby but I'm going back inside now."

Trouble knew trouble when he saw it. Viva was not going to magically appear to dry his tears. He turned on his heels and walked home, sobbing in the freezing rain.

Coco said goodbye to her fancy friends and walked alone back to the Satyricon, where Angel was coming to collect her. She swapped stories with the barkeep over a whiskey soda until her escort arrived.

"Happy New Year, baby," Angel said, full of love, as he wrapped his arms around her and kissed her.

Coco was happy to see him. Really happy. He was familiar and warm and true on this cold dark night. He loved her and was devoted to her, and he wanted so little in return. She was, she realized, devoted to him.

Coco retrieved her bag from the green room, got the band's money from the door, and walked arm-in-arm with Angel all the way up deserted Broadway the thirty blocks home. The cats clamored for attention as she took off the wig, peeled off the boots and fake eyelashes, pulled the electrical tape off her nipples. Purring contentedly, she slid into the bath Angel had run for her.

There is a time and a place for angst and confusion. But not—praise Jesus—if you're Coco Cobra.

Bridges are for Jumping

The new millennium dawned clear and cold. I bundled up and set out for Trouble's lair to do what I knew must be done.

Our affair was tearing us both apart. Trouble wanted more than I could give him, and I wanted out. My heart still yearned to be with him, but I was adept at denying my heart. Plus this would be good practice; if I could leave Trouble, I could leave Angel. Then I could leave Portland.

Trouble lived in a loft in the Eastside industrial district. I walked briskly through downtown, across the Hawthorne Bridge, and along the train tracks where the bums and hobos were just beginning to stir. I wondered if they made New Year's resolutions. If they did I bet they were the same as mine: to get the hell out of Dodge.

Trouble buzzed me in and greeted me at his door. He looked terrible. "I love you but I can't take this anymore. I'm losing my fucking mind."

I walked silently past him to the couch and perched on the arm of it, purposefully putting distance between us. "We're both losing our minds. We need to stop."

He started to cry. "I can't stop. I'm in love with you. I've been everywhere and I've never met anyone like you. You're the only reason I'm still in this fucking town. Look at me! I've been up all night weeping. It's untenable! I never shed tears over women. You've ruined me."

"I'm sorry. I thought I could do it—leave this place with you. But I'm not ready to be someone else's partner. I don't want to be anyone's partner. I want to be alone. I'm completely deranged. I need to figure out for myself what comes next."

Trouble wept silently. I moved closer to him on the couch and kissed his wet cheeks. My resolve cracked.

"I'm sorry. I'm sorry. I'm sorry. I love you madly. Let me leave Angel. The holidays are over now and I know I can do it. Give me a month. Date some other sluts. I'll be back for you, I promise."

We sat on the couch for a while in silence, listening to jazz on his turntable. Finally I bundled myself back up and headed for the freight elevator.

"I love you, Trouble. Don't ever doubt it."

God, Viva. Such a pussy. I walked towards the skate park under the Burnside Bridge. There were only a few diehards skating due to the cold. I stopped and watched them, admiring their strength and grace, until my feet turned into bricks of ice. Then I headed for the bridge.

The winter light made a splendid impressionist painting of the entire town. The river was a silvery pink, the West Hills soft and gray in the distance. Pigeons boomeranged across Burnside, from the White Stag sign to the Salvation Army shelter and back again. My heart hurt and I wasn't exactly sure why. It was more than just Trouble. Why did

I have to change anything anyway? My life was pretty excellent. I had love, money, health, respect, creative freedom. Why couldn't I just rest on my laurels for a year or two?

The thought made me shiver. Resting on laurels was not permissible. My Portland story had hit its climax and it was time for me to craft its ending.

I tried in earnest to ditch Angel later that month. I told him I never loved him and that we had to split up. He asked if there was somebody else. I said no way. He asked if I'd like to go out for dessert and a movie. I said okay. And so our charade continued. The next day I bought Trouble a copy of *Another Side of Bob Dylan*, the one with "It Ain't Me Babe" on it.

I was stuck, powerless to change a damn thing. And between the two boys, the two bands, and the two jobs I was spread too thin. I was on the verge of a nervous breakdown. I needed a break.

In my desk drawer I kept a small accordion folder where I stashed away cash for bills and rent. It was also where I kept my travel fund, which by now had nearly three thousand dollars in it. The time had come to spend it.

Heartbroken and hungry for rebirth, I left town for six weeks, hoping for death or enlightenment. I went to Paris alone. Went to Spain alone. Took the ferry to Tangiers alone and a bus to Casablanca alone. I saw a lot of great art alone. I ate a lot of bad food alone. Because I was always alone, I was frequently stalked by asshole men, so I took to spending long nights alone in my dingy hotel rooms, reading *Anna Karenina*. I felt I'd found a kindred spirit. The woman merely wanted too much. I envied her fate, however, thinking death on the train tracks sounded a lot easier than my lonesome road, spurning suitors by running around the world only to feel completely betrayed that now I had to endure my own company.

Clearly there wasn't a miracle cure or errant knight who was going to make everything all right. I'd have to overhaul my life. Myself. I had only one idea about how to do this: kill Viva Las Vegas. I owed it to my fans. Better to burn out than fade away, right? After six weeks of solitude in exotic locales, I returned to the storied West with a steely resolve. My days were numbered. They *had* to be. I would make sure they were.

But instead of planning my escape, I sank into an intractable depression. Trouble had limped back to San Francisco to lick his wounds, so there was no one to distract me from myself. My hope for a new career in film was derailed when Lyon knocked up his old lady and our movie was shelved. I was about to turn twenty-six and felt stuck in my dead-end job and dead-end relationship. I knew I wanted to be done with Viva, but what was I supposed to do instead? When you don't know what you want, there's no figuring out how to get it. I sat paralyzed at my kitchen table for much of the summer, trying to make sense of the past so I could plot the future. Meanwhile, down at the Magic Gardens, everything was going straight to hell.

Somehow during my six weeks abroad, a dark spell had fallen. Girls were addicted to coke and smack, friends were enemies, enemies were sleeping together. The resident demons of Chinatown had snuck in the door during my absence and set up shop. It was eerie how quickly everything had changed.

So many forms of escape: love, travel, drugs, death. Suddenly it seemed that everybody wanted out. Some said it had something to do with Jupiter. Whatever the case, people started dropping like flies. By Thanksgiving ten people were dead.

How to Strip, Part Five

Say your dude strangles you half to death as you're leaving for work after you call off your engagement. Or perhaps you found out he's fucking your best friend. Anyway, you've been crying for hours, your eyes are nearly swollen shut, and your heart is broken beyond repair. Or maybe it's just your ankle that's broken. Still the show must go on.

Say the phone rings, the bartender gives a sharp yelp, then tells you through tears as you're headed for the dressing room that Jessica's dead. Christian's dead. Gabrielle's dead. What are you going to do?

The only thing you can do: foundation, blush, powder. Waterproof eyeliner, waterproof mascara. Lipstick. Music. Smile.

EULOGY
"The Gospel According to Viva Las Vegas"
(Exotic Magazine, *December 2000)*

Hurtling towards the obvious, eh moonlight lady? You can try to prevent it, forget about it, derail it….but we are all indeed hurtling towards the obvious. Our paths are set, and no amount of mind shrinkage, drug drinking or soul fucking is gonna change it. I'm hurtling towards luminous, murderous mediocrity. And you? Here's derailing it: jump off a bridge, or an eight-story parking ramp for that matter. Take charge.

This year the obvious came and stole lots of people I knew and loved. Before they left, they seemed just one of us, the usual mortal slime. But once they were plucked from the now, they began to take on this ghastly destined-to-die...they were NOT like us. They were too beautiful, too kind, too sensitive. Their hearts literally too big, too easily wounded.

I depend upon people to come in and fuck my shit up. Drugs are too predictable. People aren't. The theologian Martin Buber said, "All real living is meeting." I couldn't agree more. I meet a LOT of people. To undermine the scourge of the obvious, I throw myself into the strangest circumstances, where I feast on the humans I meet. Sometimes I even love them, but I try not to. TOO GODDAMN DANGEROUS. But the sneaky bastards can get under your skin!!

I am an anthropologist by schooling and by disposition. We are an intentionally dispossessed lot, always observing communities, families, cultures, and yearning to belong. But we don't allow ourselves to fit in, because that undermines our dispassionate observational skills, our compulsive ideology of FREEDOM.

But freedom's just another word for nothing left to lose. Down at the Magic Gardens, I managed to get entangled in spite of myself. Who knew that in the bowels of a Chinatown in the goldrush newWest was a little community where I inexplicably belonged? For four years now I've been snaking around there, paying homage to nicotine and Jim Beam. Lots of people pass through the joint, some stay forever. But man it's quite a spoonful who started out year 2000 with us and just ain't around no more.

In the spring, LA Kid and his Girl did a nouveau Romeo and Juliet à la stupid fucking horse. Same pony ride left a great bass player and a beautiful punk rock girl cold on the floor. Michael and Alexa were killed in the fall by their own beautiful hearts. And last month Christian, our beloved bartender and everyone's best friend, died choking on those country-fried songs he loved, worshipped and was ... with his boots on.

If only we could have this year's Christmas bash with the ghosts of Christmas past!

But we're too busy, hurtling towards the obvious.

Here in front of me, standing on the corner, is the ghost of Christmas now. A Mexican in tight jeans, gorgeous alligator boots, a long black mane and wrap-around sunglasses. Chewing gum cockily as he walks up Burnside into the sunset. Chewing gum and strutting in the face of certain ruin. Draped in vanity and soul, walking upright in spite of the weight of the world, which is something like thirty-two feet per second, which is really very, very heavy when you think about it. He's hurtling towards the obvious, and doesn't even seem to care! The BALLS.

Here's to you, ballsy pimp-dressin' dude. In the new year I wanna follow you into the sunset. You've got it down. I'll not laugh in the face of death necessarily, but clad myself in gorgeous armour, the trappings of life. Every moment is so precious that it can be overwhelming. So I'll try not to think on it, but celebrate in minutiae: codes of dress, a swagger and a cowboy hat. Four-inch heels to the grocery store. Why the hell not?

When people die, they haunt the familiar, and occupy huge psychic spaces with their ghosts. It makes the world around you look a little less real.

But I'll tell you what's real: pink snakeskin high-heeled sandals that make matching little pink puffy scars in your feet. Somebody bought me some in the dead of winter. He's inscrutable. They aren't. They are real.

Here's to 2001 and gum-chewing (getting hitched, having babies) in the face of doom. And, if I could ask for one thing, let the black angel's death song play on away from my little life a while. I promise I'll be good.

Losing ten people in one small, close-knit work family is genocide. The first five can be blamed on karma, bad luck, bad heroin. But ten?

When Christian died in late October a funereal pall engulfed the Magic completely. Christian was Magic's bartender and resident angel. He died from his alcoholism at age twenty-fucking-nine.

Christian was from Tennessee. There is some dictate there that an honorable death involves a bottle in your hand and boots on your feet. He always wore cowboy shirts over his Misfits t-shirts, skinny jeans, and cowboy boots. He had a rebel flag tattooed on his right arm and went to great lengths to explain that he wasn't racist, it was just part of his heritage. He and his identical twin brother were fixtures in the punk rock scene. Several of us strippers had dated him. He was a walking Hank Williams song.

The night Christian died was the night of the Clown Parade. One of Magic's bouncers, Abraham, had a Clown Parade every year to celebrate his birthday. Dozens of strippers and hipsters dressed up as clowns to go barhopping all over town. It was a gas-gas-gas. His last night on earth, Christian was dressed for the festivities: black-and-white striped and polka-dotted baggy clown suit, curly wig, *Clockwork Orange* face paint, and a big red clown nose. All the clowns convened at the Magic and walked across 4th Avenue to Hung Far Low.

Christian was acting strange. People thought he was drunk. He vomited black blood on the linoleum floor of the cavelike bar and was asked to leave. Friends packed him into a cab and sent him home to sleep it off. Half an hour later, he called the Magic. His voice was almost indiscernible, only a gurgle. Terri handed the phone to Big Steve, his best friend. Christian was begging for help. Cab Driver Bill, Drunk Paul, and Big Steve piled into Bill's cab and sped to Christian's house. Steve found him. He was already dead. He had choked on his vomit.

After Christian's death we just couldn't get it back together. The Magic was cursed. It was anyone's guess who'd be the next to check out.

Sweet Melissa—a stunning redhead who'd replaced Rain as the reigning belle of Chinatown—had suffered a terrible breakup and subsequent miscarriage and sought solace in the needle. Already she'd OD'd a handful of times and was such a junkie that she came into the Magic with her dealers, covered in sores, hoping for a handout from one of her former admirers. She'd sold everything she had and was trading blowjobs for drugs. She was skin and bones, a walking cadaver. We were just waiting for that phone call to commence our grieving in earnest.

Siri, Magic's remaining weekend starlet, was in prison. She was arrested naked onstage for a felony drug rap after a meth lab was discovered at her house. The mandatory minimum for her crime was twelve years. She went AWOL to Baltimore, but eventually her past caught up with her. She got lucky and only had to serve six months, but six months in federal prison can be hard on a girl. Siri was gutted pretty thoroughly and was out for another year before she got her spark back.

I had to leave. I didn't care where, when, or how. Again I had the feeling that my story had already climaxed and that by not leaving I was botching it badly. I wasn't playing music anymore and my *Exotic* columns had become a roadmap of my depression. Who the hell'd want to read that?

I had to leave, had to burn these sad bridges.

Gotta Get Away

Depression sucks. It seems so indulgent, so very selfish. Of course life is hard. Of course people die. Of course you can't always get what you want. But the depressive takes these facts of life personally, as if the universe's laws were created just to vex her. Someone famously said that depression equals reality divided by expectations. Which means that dreamers like me are doomed.

I had tried so hard to be content in paradise. I tried to convince myself that the affectionate codependence I felt for Johnny Angel was enough for me, was "love." I tried hard to effect change, too, hoping that if I went "straight," headed back to grad school and became a professor, maybe the blues would fade. I finally took the Foreign Service exam and aced it. I read self-help books like *Wishcraft* and *What Color is My Parachute,* hoping to deduce my optimal occupational future. Maybe I could stay in Portland, in my lovely, cozy home, if Portland had a job for me that I liked and thought worthy of me, a job other than stripping. Not that I didn't love stripping; I did, with all my heart. But I had definitely hit the glass ceiling. There was nowhere to go but down or out.

The career counsel I sought from self-help books only confirmed that stripping was my ideal occupation. I needed a stage whereupon I could speak my own truth. Not even acting would let me do that. I needed art, music, and like-minded outlaw souls. Where could I find these things away from Magic Gardens? Where might my peculiar skill set command a living wage? Music and publishing were industries I thought I could stand. And there was only one place to go for that combo.

New York.

That December I headed east for four days to see if I could hack it. As I took the bus from Newark to New York City, winding through grimy neighborhoods and old factory parks, I remembered how much I hated the East Coast. So much of it is old, cold, hidebound, and tacky. What the fuck was I doing?

The bus spit me out at Penn Station. It was freezing and quickly getting dark. I walked with my giant backpack all the way down 8th Avenue to Jane Street where, smack in the middle of the ultra-posh West Village, was a perfectly awful hostel. When Lonely Planet describes a place as a transient hotel, it's best to take note and avoid it. It *was* a transient hotel. It stank, was filthy and flea-ridden, and the resident transients were a lot scarier than any West Coast bums I had met.

My room was a musty dusty cell, so small that the twin bed would only fit at an angle. There was a single window that looked out onto an airshaft. It let in no daylight, but the neon lights from the stairwells shone in brighter than day all night.

I couldn't sleep. I could hear my neighbors roll over, could hear the proverbial pin drop, could hear the fleas flocking excitedly towards my flesh. I pounded my pillow, furious at my insistence to uproot myself from the verdant valleys of the West where I was loved and cared for, to strand myself alone and lonely in shitty hotels all over the world. Paris, Barcelona, Casablanca, Berlin, Bali. Furious at my insistence to maroon myself permanently in the dirty cold concrete jungle of New York City. Furious at my proclivity to always and forever break my own heart.

The first morning I cried for several hours and then headed out into the cold crisp air. I comforted myself with a chocolate cannoli and *caffè Americano* at Bruno's Bakery on Bleecker Street. That revived me considerably. I bought a peppermint candle, eyemask, earplugs, and aspirin at a Duane Reade and several tangerines from a fruit market in SoHo in an effort to make my tenement more like Van Gogh's garret.

I walked around the city to the point of utter exhaustion. Around eight in the evening I had two Maker's Mark manhattans to knock me out, collapsed in my filthy, flea-ridden bed and slept for twelve hours. The next morning I awoke mildly euphoric. New York was playing chess with my insides. And winning, of course.

I went to the Museum of Natural History, saw *Cabaret* at Studio 54, and caught a glorious folk punk band in the East Village. I made myself a regular at a greasy Chinese noodle joint in Hell's Kitchen. I flirted with cops and kissed a Sagittarius stranger because it was his birthday. Then I skipped home through the snow.

New York has Tinkerbell dust all over it. It's a parable of beauty and salvation. I arrived shipwrecked, desolate, desperate, and heartbroken and, four days later, left SAVED, my depression evaporated into a heady headstrong fortitude and with a certainty that I could and would transcend Portland. It was nothing short of a miracle.

On the eve of my departure, homeward bound to the boy and the bars, I huddled on the banks of the Hudson on a bitterly cold night. The Statue of Liberty stood proud in the distance, promising freedom. A huge orange moon sank slowly into New Jersey. I said a prayer.

"Please bring me to this wonderful city. Please help me to arrange my affairs, and to have the courage to say the goodbyes. And the next time I set foot on this island, let me be moving here."

I tingled with excitement. The stars twinkled approvingly in the cold winter sky. Something had changed in my heart. It had come unmoored, finally, from the gorgeous lagoon of Strip City.

I returned from New York lit up like Christmas, with post-orgasmic languor and liveliness. I had a wildly impossible goal—my favorite thing—and I trained my crazy brain on it with my faith once again intact.

I tried to keep it quiet, though. Partly I didn't want to deal with the goodbyes. I wanted to burn as brightly as I always had, then one day vanish. Leave 'em really hanging, high and dry, haunted by the void I'd left. Also, I feared Terri. If Terri knew I was cutting the tethers, she might shaft me totally on shifts. I had no money saved, and had yet to pay off Africa, NYC, and Christmas. I was moving to New York where a thousand dollars would last me one day. I figured I needed at least a thousand dollars.

So it was business as usual. Except now I wore an I ❤ NY t-shirt twice a night, dancing to Blondie, Lou Reed, the Velvet Underground, the Ramones, the Heartbreakers, the New York Dolls, the Jim Carroll Band. And I was still lit up like Christmas through January, February, March, when no one else was.

* * *

TO: Viva "Everything I Needed To Know About Life I Learned From The Ramones" Las Vegas, Contributing Editor
RE: JOYEUX NOEL

Dearest Viva:
"AN INDECENT CHRISTMAS TO US ALL!" As I was looking over what I guess passes for Exotic Magazine's Holiday Issue, I was expecting to find another of your delightful 'Twas the Night Before Christmas parodies that we've all grown so accustomed to this time of year. I happen to be very fond of your annual jab at poetry, not only 'cos it is an exemplum of Holiday Spirit, but it's also a welcome break from your usual fare of bragging about showing off your panties to shoeshine boys, or cynicism such as the kind you demonstrated against our fine Olympic athletes. Um, actually...all kidding aside, I really think your "Eulogy" article this month was the best work I've ever seen you do. Really, really excellent writing. Your article was a tough, so-bering, yet tender exploration of the fragility of the now. It was complete, in-tense, heartfelt, and beautiful. It also totally blew away anything that I've ever seen written in Exotic before. Really excellent work, Viva.
While interviewing Laurie Holmes (hey, go ahead and laugh, but there were a lot of people who tried to get her to commit to doing a screenplay, and out of all of them I was the only one able to break through and get it done), she suggested I contact a longtime friend of John's named Bill Margold. Bill had directed both John and Laurie in a 1983 gem titled California Valley Girls, and when I finally did talk to him I basically wanted to know one thing: How much does it cost to get a John Holmes? He told me, "$1,500 cash." When I said that wasn't a bad payoff for one day's work, he shouted, "What do you mean by a day's work? He wasn't even there for two hours. He pretty much just showed up, got a blowjob, then left!" Initially, I had thought of John as a man with extremely simple tastes. You know, one of these guys who would be happy as long as he had enough drugs for the day and a couch to crash on, but

man, if he had TWO COUCHES and drugs for all his loser friends, then he would be stylin'. The real truth, I now suspect, is far more complicated than that. John certainly must have known that his name on a porno box cover would guarantee huge sales, yet he never once tried to license his name, his fame. He never owned his own home, had children, or seemed to care about holding any stake in this society whatsoever. His self-effacing, marginal lifestyle actually recalls William S. Burroughs, who put himself through Harvard, then found work as (among other things) a door-to-door salesman. Or Jack Kerouac, who graduated from Columbia University, then got a job as a night watchman. It also reminds me of another person I know... graduate of Williams College... BA in anthropology... and now undresses at a club located in a part of town where most good people roll up their windows and make sure the car doors are locked anytime they dare venture through it.

Yeah, yeah, I've heard all of your arguments about "easy money," and how you're not tied down to a 40-hour a week schedule, but I'm not sure I'm buying it. Too many things about your background don't fit with your choosing to become a stripper. It doesn't fit, like your hands don't fit around the fretboard of a Fender Stratocaster. You have these tiny little hands. I remember watching you playing on stage and wondering how you could manage to make any of the chords. Your hands were not made for playing rock & roll, chain smoking, and downing shots in strip clubs. Your hands were made for teaching class, or for putting Band-Aids on children's ouwies.

Despite all that, you created this identity for yourself, and have been quite successful at everything you've tried. And I'm sure when you move on to the next chapter of your life, you will be equally successful. After all, you've got a pretty impressive track record of making things happen, so far. I am so impressed at how you did not go down that safe, familiar road of job, marriage, and family. Not that there's anything wrong with that, of course, it's just that it would have been too easy for you. Yet, as you know, this sort of "freedom" has its own price tag. "Dancers work for tips only," yeah, that and a lot more. I truly do admire you. I know I would never have had the courage to do the things that you have done.

And so, Viva, I'm wishing you all the best for the upcoming New Year. As for me, my next project is finding Kasey Kola (this is the gal who made a suicide pact with Germs leadsinger, Darby Crash... and survived, of course), and see if I can put together a script around her story and 1979 Los Angeles. Hope you enjoy the Rock & Roll Penis Chart I've sent you this year (yes, my dear, REAL rock groupies have e-mailed this site with the real deal on some of your favorite rock stars). Give my love to Teresa and Miss Mona, and (dare I say it to all you sophisticated, cynical types?) "Merry Christmas!"

Sincerely yours, Alan O.

P.S. Glad to see Jim Goad has arrived at Exotic *just in time to vomit all over your Christmas stockings!*

Life is a Cabaret

My new year dawned gray and misty on the mean streets of Seattle, in a van amongst my favorite rock 'n' roll band, Zen Guerrilla. I was supposed to have worked New Year's Eve at the Magic, but Terri no longer had a stranglehold on my life now that I was leaving, and I cancelled my shift without one tiny frisson of guilt. I called in sick and hopped the 8 PM train to Seattle, arriving just in time to ring in the New Year with my band boys at the OK Hotel. We stayed up all night, ate breakfast at Shari's, then headed back to the train station.

So it was that I had three crystalline hours to consider the year 2001 as the Amtrak Cascade made its way along the bay towards Olympia. Puget Sound was impossibly beautiful in the morning light. All sorts of critters busied themselves with breakfast. Herons stood knee-deep near shore, fishing, as stout fish broke the glassy pink surface of the water further out, hunting for bugs. I was tired after a night of dancing, drinking, and flirting, but felt more content than I could ever remember feeling.

New York. Hopefully by spring. Three months would give me enough time to find a place to live, stockpile a bit of cash, and tie up loose ends at home. Then I'd take Manhattan. My plan was to rededicate my life to rock 'n' roll. I'd ditch my cats, my car, my piano, my lover, all my trappings of domesticity, and leave town like I came in: with the clothes on my back and a guitar. Except now I had three guitars. Fuck it. I'd take them all. I'd find a job once I got out there. How hard could

MISS MONA'S LADIES of LEISURE

FEATURING THE FON-DELLS

JUNE 29
SUNDAY 10 PM

SPECIAL GUEST
SPECTATOR PUMP

PARTIAL PROCEEDS
BENEFIT THE INVISIBLE
FRINGE ADULT ENTERTAINERS
COLLECTIVE

BERBATI'S PAN

231 SOUTHWEST ANKENY • 248-4579

it be? I could bartend. I'd been editing a magazine for three years. I had alumni connections that actually meant something back East. And of course I could always get naked for money. (Or at least strip down to a G-string. New York didn't allow full nudity in bars.)

Johnny was incredibly supportive of the idea. He only wanted to see me happy and was thrilled that my stubborn depression seemed to have lifted. He planned to move out and join me after his first year of law school wrapped. Of course he didn't know I was leaving him for good. How could he when I couldn't even admit it to myself?

I drifted off to sleep somewhere in central Washington, world's happiest kitten, dressed in a short red satin *cheongsam* and knee-high patent-leather boots, basking in the weak winter sun, dreaming of the bright future. Once again I felt the certainty that everything would work out. How could it not, when already 2001 was off to such a great start?

By the end of January I'd found an apartment through the grapevine and set a date for my departure: March 21. I'd take the train. That way I could bring a couple bags of clothes, most of my shoe collection, three guitars, and my bicycle. I spent a day at Kinko's photocopying every piece of writing I'd ever published for a clipbook and commissioned one of the computer geeks from Magic to build me a website. I had headshots done by a photographer friend, in case any movie work happened my way in NYC. All that stood between me and my new life was two rocks shows, two modeling gigs, one issue of *Exotic*, and one final cabaret.

A gal named Lucy Fur was producing her second cabaret. Because Mona was happily ensconced in Boston, a whole continent away, working as a secretary (untenable) and living with a man she called her fiancé (even worse), I figured that meant I was free to perform in rival cabarets (although I stopped short of telling Mo about it).

Lucy's first cabaret was her 20th Century Underwear Revue, featuring girls stripping down to unmentionables from each decade. I got lucky and got to represent the sixties, dressed in my Coco wig, flower-power polyester panties, and a cotton bra that easily caught fire when I doused it with lighter fluid and struck a match. This year Lucy was producing a Comic Book Cabaret, starring strippers dressed as Rainbow Brite, Strawberry Shortcake, Wonder Woman, Aeon Flux, Cheetarah,

Sailor Moon, and more. Lucy made the elaborate costumes herself, hired drag queens to do hair and makeup, and provided all the soundtracks. Each character performed a campy set, then go-go danced on catwalks and stages while a DJ spun records. While it wasn't a Miss Mona Cabaret, it was silly, sexy, and a hell of a lot of fun.

Lucy asked me to front the house band: Josie and the Pussycats. For this purpose I recruited another favorite rock 'n' roll band, Scared of Chaka, to back me up on lead guitar and drums. All three of us sported "long tails, and ears for hats," just like the 'toon's title track, which we covered, in addition to Joan Jett's "Bad Reputation," Detroit Cobras' "Bad Girl," VOM's "Too Animalistic," and, for a bit of variety (or perhaps because I'd inconveniently fallen in love with Chaka's guitar player), Mickey and Sylvia's "Love is Strange." Our twelve-minute set of perfect punk pop was among the best twelve minutes of my life. And a fitting swan song to Portland, I thought—a bunch of bona fide characters reveling in absurdity, booze, and skin.

The high after the show lasted a week, the hangover only twelve hours. But there was no sleeping it off. My final column for *Exotic* was due the next day, so I was up by 9 AM, swam twenty laps to stretch my sore muscles, then headed to Huber's, Portland's oldest bar, to write.

"The Gospel According to Viva Las Vegas"
(Exotic Magazine, *March 2001)*

> The devil is the spirit of gravity.
> He who is not a bird should not build his nest over abysses.
> —Nietzsche, *Thus Spoke Zarathustra*

Too true, too true. The devil is the spirit of gravity. I've been here nearly five years. FIVE YEARS. A personal record. Often I've felt that it was gravity keeping me here. The DEVIL. But I am a bird. I can fly. Ain't been stretchin' my wings much lately, tho' (you noticed?). So, before they atrophy and I die in a lonely bridge-jump, I'm burnin' down the house. Cuz the obvious extrapolation from the above quotes is how do you know if you're a bird if you don't challenge the spirit of gravity? If you don't live over an abyss?

So, Portland, I gotta go. Though it breaks my heart to say it. I become too complacent if I'm in one place for too long. In my life I've mastered this trick.

I call it the Phoenix. Once I've ridden roughshod over all the hearts and hillocks I wanna, then I've no choice but to set it all aflame. Burn the bridges, burst the bubbles. And like the mythical Phoenix, rise from the ashes.

I guess my destination is New York town. I got a bass player out there. And a million friends. My only goal is to make y'all proud.

'Course I do owe you a lot, Portland. I mean, when I arrived back in '96, I didn't know how to drink at a bar, didn't know how to carry a purse, had never seen eyeliner or owned naughty shoes, never tasted a manhattan or let someone buy me a drink. I've totally fallen in love with so much of you, so many of you. Hell, Old Town is the fifth chamber of my heart.

Right now I'm suckin' down a Marlboro Light and chit-chattin' with an alcoholic elder at Huber's ("#1 Kahlua sales in Oregon"), where I've conquered the demon writer's block many times with one or two Spanish coffees. And let y'all see me ALL nude. Strikes me as funny, how stripping can be so intimate, yet so superficial. I've bared a hell of a lot more in these little columns. Viva's cocky "WHAT I KNOW," "WHAT I WANT," and "I SPEAK THE TRUTH." And ya know, I've been sifting through the past three years of musings, and I must say my opinions have not changed:

1. Rock 'n' Roll should make your panties wet.

2. Zen Guerrilla rocks the MOST.

3. Stripping is art.

This older gal down the bar from me is butting into my column, all lubed-up with vodka sodas, tipping quarters, and imperiously demanding of the bartender,

"Gavin! A match! I've read everything on this box (Marlboro Lights), Gavin, and it says 'Made in the U.S.A.'"

"Richmond, Virginia."

"They have the best horses there. I read somewhere that that's where Queen Elizabeth vacations to buy horses."

Anyway, I'd like to further investigate the above truths in the next few years. And it looks like I'll be reporting back to y'all from the front, as Exotic *has asked me to keep up the good work, albeit from the other coast. I think maybe I'll change the title, though, from "The Gospel" to "Sex in the City." Oh, YEAH.*

"Gavin! How do you spell eenie meenie minie moe?"

"I try not to very often. I'd rather spell supercalifragilisticexpialadocious, ya know?"

"Well, you're educated."

This is a great town. Don't think I don't think so. It's just...the abyss... the abyss is calling me.

And once more with feeling, ZEN GUERRILLA, motherfuckers!!

Glow Girl

My March column for *Exotic* let the cat out of the bag. I was deserting and wasn't nobody gonna stop me. An alarm rang out through the strip community and lots of long-time-no-sees came in for a last dance while my day planner filled with appointments for goodbye cocktails.

The evening of my very last shift at the Magic, I met Richard Meltzer for farewell wine and whiskey at Dot's on Clinton Street. Richard was among the most esteemed elders in the rock 'n' roll world and I'd interviewed him for *Exotic* in January. A rock critic and musician, he was Yale-educated, published the very first review of Jimi Hendrix, palled around with the Dictators, Patti Smith, and Lester Bangs, and, most importantly, wrote like a motherfucker. Johnny Angel hero-worshipped Meltzer, and I was a disciple, too. Richard and I became friends during the course of the three-hour *Exotic* interview, which occurred at his home so I could help him administer dialysis to his geriatric cat. Sadly this was mere months before I flew the coop, but I adored hanging out with Meltzer and took plenty of time off from packing to hear his firsthand tales of rock 'n' roll Babylon.

On our final date at Dot's, Richard passed me a little square of paper. On it were four numbers.

"Those are the only friends I have left who've stuck around that go-dawful place. I don't know why they don't get the fuck out. It's a hellhole. But give 'em a call. They might be able to throw you a bone or somethin'."

My eyes widened in disbelief. "Tosches as in Nick Tosches? The famous writer? Handsome Dick Manitoba from the Dictators?" These guys were Angel's gods, and I'd read and heard about them for years.

"Yup. I dunno what Manitoba could help you with, but I think he runs a bar or somethin'. Liza's this crazy Jewish broad I used to run around with. She's a writer. Used to date Bukowski."

"Wow. Awesome! Who's Chuck?"

"Some guy at the *Village Voice*. Chuck Eddy. I don't know that I've ever met him. He wrote *Stairway to Hell*. He likes my writing."

"Holy shit! The hundred best heavy metal bands of all time? That *Stairway to Hell*?"

"How do you know all these books, baby? Don't you know that rock 'n' roll will spoil your brain? You laugh but I'm serious. I haven't listened to that shit since the late sixties. It's all crap. You should listen to jazz."

"Oh horseshit, Richard. You love it. Your home is a fuckin' monument to rock 'n' roll. You wrote half the lyrics for the Blue Öyster Cult, for Christ's sake. Don't tell me you don't listen to rock."

"I'm just tellin' you cuz it's true. That shit'll rot your brain."

"Whatever. Richard, thank you SO MUCH for these numbers. You really think it's okay if I call these people?"

"Sure. Why not? You've got that glow thing goin' on. I bet that anyone wasting away in that garbage dump would be happy to get a call from you. Tell 'em I say hello. I haven't talked to 'em in years."

I kissed the square of paper and carefully tucked it into my cigarette compact. I'd lost a hundred cocktail napkins with phone numbers on them. I was not going to lose this one. I felt like I'd been given a key to the City, four friends-of-a-friend who might magically orient my compass on an island of eight million strangers. I hugged Richard tightly and promised I'd keep in touch. I paid our tab and then steered my Volvo back downtown to Old Town for my last shift at the Magic. Ever.

You Gotta Move

There was a manhattan waiting for me at the end of the bar when I arrived.

"Is this for me?" I asked Terri. I was the only one who regularly drank manhattans, but I figured I'd better ask to be safe.

"Yes. That's from Mr. Anonymous," replied Terri in her squeaky mouse voice. Mr. Anonymous had died the year before from a heart attack. Could it be that Terri had actually bought me a drink?

"Thank you, Mr. Anonymous!" I raised my glass in salute to the heavens and took a nip. Terri hugged me.

"We're going to miss you, Viva."

Suddenly it seemed a softball had lodged in my throat.

"Oh Terri. Stop it. Now someone else can use the martini glass," I said, maintaining my composure. The Magic Gardens only owned one martini glass. The rest had broken and they were evidently too expensive to replace. I took another slug of bourbon, then hustled down to the basement to get ready.

I pulled out my makeup bag and set it on the vanity, rummaged through my giant backpack, and plucked out my pink leopard short shorts, groovy striped thong, and Scared of Chaka t-shirt the Pussycats' drummer had screened for me. I smeared tangerine-scented glitter lotion all over my body, the armor that steeled me for battle, got dressed, and applied an indelible coat of Revlon Vixen lipstick. I browsed through my CDs and selected the Sonics, the Sweet, Royal Trux, and some early Stones. All this was so familiar. I had gone through the same motions over and over again, same outfit, same songs, yet somehow it never got old. Every night was a different audience and a different dance. Every night some pearl of wisdom would fall from the lips of an accidental angel—perhaps the guy fresh out of twenty years in prison, perhaps the man from Boston with his collar shirt and khakis, maybe the other dancer, maybe me. God I loved stripping.

I sauntered back upstairs, more slowly now that I was wearing my seven-inch leopard platforms. I programmed my music as Kitty picked up the dollars from her final dance of the evening, then sipped on my manhattan to still the butterflies in my stomach—my last night!—as the tinny guitar intro of the Sonics' "Cinderella" rang through the bar. I minced my way to the stage, greeting admirers and shaking hands. It felt like a fucking political rally at times, except that when I got to the stage, instead of making a speech I started dancing around and posing. Sometimes it took as much as thirty seconds before my self-consciousness evaporated and I was in the zone, enough time to wonder *What the fuck am I doing onstage? Why are these people watching me? Why am I wearing this ridiculous outfit?* But finally the music and the movement would focus me and I'd be on for the rest of the night. It was so addictive. A salve! Sometimes I wished I could be onstage every minute of my life, to always live in the moment and stop fucking thinking and brooding. Thank God they had stages in New York City.

Before I knew it the Ritalin rock of the Stones' "Have You Seen Your Mother Baby, Standing in the Shadow?" was careening to a close. I was naked. I picked up my money and thanked everyone for supporting the arts, then slipped into my robe to mingle with the crowd for a few minutes. Then I scampered back to the basement to prepare for my next set. The other gal's songs whizzed by so fast. I barely had enough time to count and face my ones and bundle them in stacks of twenty, get re-dressed, touch up my makeup, put away CDs, pick new ones, then hustle back upstairs to chat over another cocktail with whoever had bought it.

More Stones, more Sweet. Ramones, Suicide, Blondie. Screamin' Jay Hawkins, Ella Fitzgerald, the Cramps. Time was flying. A dozen hard-core fans made appearances, bearing gifts of dog-eared Kerouac and Plato, rare orchids, a fifth of Knob Creek, each desiring my undivided attention. Onstage I was the heartbreaker, offstage the hostess. It was exhausting but really I was so good at it. It occurred to me mid-striptease that I was leaving in my prime, but I had no regrets. Don't look back.

I kept my eyes on the clock. As we neared closing time, I prepared for my last set. While Tabitha the Scandinavian princess pranced around in her polka-dotted panties, I stepped out into the foyer with Abe the bouncer.

"Are you sad, Viva?"

"Not really. You know, I don't think I'm gonna miss stripping. I feel ready to be done. But what I am gonna miss...."

I opened the door to the street and stepped outside in my short black velvet dress and knee-high black leather boots and wistfully took a last look at 2 AM Chinatown. The decrepit buildings stood stark against the starless steel-gray sky. Neon from the House of Louie and the Republic Café illuminated the mist in pink and gold. Street lamps formed pools of light on the oily rain-slicked street.

"...is this."

Two minutes later I was spinning around stage to Iggy Pop's "Lust for Life." Then "Trash" by the New York Dolls followed by "Time Has Come Today" by the Chambers Brothers.

"Alright boys and girls, this is it!" I yelled from stage. "My last song ever!"

"Viva! Viva!" They were actually chanting. I was mortified and blushed deep purple. Keith Richards came to my rescue, picking the bluesy opening of "You Gotta Move." The butterflies were back with a vengeance. It felt like they would spirit me away. But I kept on dancing.

"...when the Lord..."

"...gets ready..."

"...you gotta move."

The End

And so my Portland tale came to an end. Well, it didn't so much come to an end as I willed it to end, and it wasn't exactly the ending I'd hoped for. For a while I thought our little band of outcasts really would save the world, wrenching folks out of their collective stupor and resuscitating their spirits, one enlightened striptease at a time. There is strength in numbers, and united it seemed like the Magic Gardens girls might be able to pull it off. But as the imperatives of adulthood and addictions

RAILROAD jerk

with

SATYRICON

april **19** SAT

THE HARLOTS   THE PRIMRODS
NEW WAVE HOOKERS

splintered us apart, we weakened considerably. On our own we couldn't quite save anything, except, with luck, ourselves.

I bought a one-way train ticket to Penn Station. It felt so familiar to bookend my life's chapters by leaving town and starting over. I'd done it ten times before, moving from parish to parish with my family, from country to country alone. I felt confident that I'd ace it this time. I'd ditch Portland, then I'd take Manhattan.

Pink took the morning off from work to meet me for coffee. We had coffee every Saturday—a ritual we'd observed for years. But this time Wednesday would have to do, cuz there'd be no more Saturdays. The thought of it made a large knot in my chest as I watched Pink approach the coffee shop.

"You all packed?" he asked as we stood in line.

"Yup. Packed, threw out half of everything, packed again. Evidently my room in Brooklyn is pretty small. But I'm bringing all my shoes."

"What are you doing with the rest of your stuff?"

"Johnny's babysitting: car, cats, computer, most of my clothes. I figure I'll fly out in the fall when I have my own apartment and know what I need. The rest I'll get rid of."

We ordered our usual, double *Americanos* and scones, and sat at our favorite table by the window. We were like a couple of old ladies, I always thought—insistent that everything be just so for our epic Saturday gossip sessions. Goddamn I was gonna miss Pink.

"I can't believe you're actually doing this," Pink sighed. He looked sad.

"I can't quite believe it either. But I gotta get out. I feel like I've done everything I can in this town. Anything beyond this is redundant. Redundancy equals death. And if Mona can get out, I can get out."

"Teresa's heading out East too, you know, for the summer."

"I know. Where's she going? Atlanta? Some harm reduction government job? That girl gets around. Hopefully we can all meet up. You, too."

Pink and I lingered as long as we could. He was my best friend and confidant and it killed me to leave him. But finally we had to say goodbye. His eyes moistened as he gave me a hug.

"Be careful out there, Viva. And keep in touch."

"I love you so much!" I whimpered. Pink turned to go. I watched him as he walked down the block, all the way back to his apartment. Then I strolled through the college campus towards home.

When I reached the highway overpass, I turned and looked back towards downtown. So this is how it ends, I thought. I was proud of all that I'd accomplished, but chastened, too. So many dreams had faded; so many people had died. Truthfully, I didn't want to get on that train. I wanted to stay in the land of milk and honey forever, surrounded by friends in a place where money literally grew on trees. But I was so tired and so bored. I couldn't let my fans see me crumble or fade. I owed it to them to ride off into the sunset on a giant white steed. Or, I owed it to my ego, my story, my stubborn allegiance to my starry-eyed side.

Later that afternoon, Johnny and I packed my several boxes, two duffel bags of clothes, three guitars, and bicycle into my Volvo for the short drive to the train station. Johnny Angel, the most mistreated man alive, hugged me tightly and then threw me millions of kisses, mouthing I-love-yous with tears in his eyes as I boarded the train. My insides were a knife fight and every breath cut me. I tried not to breathe. Swallowed sobs. Johnny Angel... This was it. I hadn't even had the balls to let him know, much less let him go.

With trembling hands I arranged my quarters. I took out my water and whiskey and my journal and pen and made sure my Walkman was set to play the soundtrack I'd prepared as we pulled out of Portland. The train lurched once and then glided slowly away from Johnny Angel, from Old Town, past the police stables and under the Broadway Bridge, red and wonderfully angular in the late afternoon sun. The knife fight escalated into an all-consuming howl.

"Stop! Let me out! I've changed my mind! Johnny Angel!"

The howl was swallowing me. I fought back with the MC5. "I Can Only Give You Everything."

I gulped down more sobs as we passed the train yards and tankers along Highway 30. Just before the St. Johns Bridge the train curved sharply and crossed the Willamette on an old black train bridge, then sped along a corridor through North Portland, over the Columbia River and into Washington. As soon as we crossed state lines the howl subsided. The end was over.

Leave the saving to the other angels, I thought. My work was done. I grabbed my pen, my steadfast companion on all the roads I'd traveled alone, and put it to paper, partly to coax some confidence, but mostly to force my new beginning.

It seems to me that to be an outlaw, to be outside the law, you have to be optimistic. Whether you're shooting pool or shooting for the moon—you gotta believe or you're never gonna make it. Outlaws walk that tightrope every night.

It's always the dreamers who stay up the latest.

Epilogue

It is May 2009 as I put the finishing touches on *Magic Gardens*. Its writing has truly been a labor of love, and love is a lot harder and more complicated than most folks guess.

My move to NYC in 2001 was everything I dreamed it would be and more. I fell hard for that town, and the events of 9/11 broke my heart. Soon after, I found myself on a westbound train back to Portland, my intention to write this book and then move back to the City. Chuck Eddy said it'd take three months. It took seven years.

In the time that's passed, I've learned a lot more about community and finally swapped my stubborn anthropological remove for membership in Portland's rag-tag band of outlaws. God willing, I'll continue to write the saga of Mona, Teresa, Viva, Pink, Rain, and friends.

Portland tends to be a rather deadly place, and, ultimately, the reason I sit in solitude at my desk day after day is because so many of our friends aren't around anymore to tell their stories. There are dozens who've split, but in particular, I'd like to thank Adam Cox, Paul Stojanovich, Lori Malisewski, and Sasha Clapper for the endless inspiration they've given me. See you on the other side.

XOXOX,
Viva Las Vegas

About the Author

Whether naked on stage at a dive bar in Portland, Oregon, or walking the red carpet at the Cannes Film Festival, Viva Las Vegas brings passion to her performances and audiences to their feet.

Born and raised in the Midwest and a graduate of Williams College in Massachusetts, Viva has been a force in the arts for more than a decade, performing onstage as a singer, appearing in TV shows and more than a dozen films, and writing and interviewing for publications both local and national. Viva's atypical resume includes *Paranoid Park* and *First Kiss* (films by Gus Van Sant); *The Auteur* (a 2008 James Westby film); and articles in *The New York Times*, *Village Voice*, *Portland Monthly*, and *Exotic Magazine*. Her Portland band, Coco Cobra and the Killers, has recorded two albums, and she is frequently interviewed as a spokesperson for strippers—her compassionate voice always at the ready to rock polite society.

Acknowledgments

Many, many people helped this book come to be. In particular, I'd like to thank Jedediah Aaker, Mary Artz, Sarah Bartlett, Rob Bonds, Jean Braden, Jay Browning, Hilary Campbell, Jesse Champlin, Andrei Codrescu, Kari Coleman, Allison Collins, Kimberly Crowell, Robyn Crummer-Olson, Jan Davis, Asha Dornfest, Lisa Douglass, Katherine Dunn, Lainie Ettinger, Frank Fallaice, Margaret Foley, Lucy Fur, Amber Geiger, Jessica Glenn, Ariel Gore, Scott Green, Caroline Griffin, Roman Gunther, Michael Hebb, Linda Hefferman, Michael Hornburg, Bo Björn Johnson, Vicki Keller, Jesse Kimball, Connie Kirk, Lori Malisewski, Dennis Mandell, Cameron Marschall, Rosie McKinlay, Richard Meltzer, Linda Meyer, Marie Miller, Everett Moore, Tylor Neist, Lee Nelson, Alan Osborn, Kristoffer Østhus, Jane Roper, Jonathan Sarre, Mona Superhero, Tiffany Talbott, Nick Tosches, Gus Van Sant, Jen Weaver-Neist, Bruce Webber, Jackie Weissman, and James Westby.

For the first Factory Girl Press edition, hats (bras, panties) off to Christopher Corbell, Jon Frisby, Kohel Haver, David Howitt, Elaine Lowry, Andy Norris, and Drew Wiltsey. Merci mille fois!

CPSIA information can be obtained at www.ICGtesting.com
Printed in the USA
BVOW06s2326161215

430494BV00038B/2211/P